AF429153

THE ISLAND

A Personal Account of Taiwan's Extraordinary Transformation

Mark O'Neill

The Island
By Mark O'Neill

ISBN-13: 978-988-8843-35-0

HISTORY / Asia

EB200

Published in Hong Kong by Earnshaw Books Ltd.

FOREWORD

The transformation of Taiwan over the last 40 years is a story worth telling. This story has greatly moved me, and I hope it will move the reader too.

In the summer of 1981, I had the great good fortune to go to the island to study the Chinese language. It was the start of a friendship both with Taiwan and its people that has lasted more than 40 years. During the first visit, I stayed for two and a half years. It was a combination of study with work as an editor and journalist to pay for the school fees and living expenses. What impressed me most was how helpful everyone was—both teachers and ordinary people. For a westerner, learning an Oriental language with a different script—like Hindi, Japanese or Chinese—is a special challenge. You need a great deal of help—and people provided it.

The situation of the island in those days was not normal. Since 1949, it had been under martial law, with one-party rule, no freedom of expression nor free media. The stated aim of the government was "to recover the mainland". But life was normal. Every morning people hurried to work and school; shops, restaurants and cinemas were full. Foreigners like me could live where we chose—in a hotel, in a hostel with Taiwan people, in our own apartment or with a local family. Many welcomed a foreign tenant—to pay rent, or perhaps replace a child who had moved out to live elsewhere in Taiwan or overseas. You could have as much contact with local people as you wished—the ideal conditions for learning a foreign language.

Over the next four decades, I have returned regularly to

Taiwan, for work, research and social visits. I have written two other books about Taiwan subjects; I have witnessed a transformation that no-one could have imagined in 1981. Today Taiwan does not have one political party, but dozens of them. Once upon a time, people were careful to repeat the official line; now everyone has a different opinion and is eager to express it. Instead of a one-party media, there are now too many — radio and television stations, social media, websites and information flooding in from abroad. There are elections to choose just about every post, from village chief to national president. During my first stay, Taiwan was noted for producing badminton racquets, gym shoes, umbrellas and T-shirts. Now it manufactures the world's most sophisticated semi-conductors and other top-of-the-market electronic and computer items. Taiwan companies have invested all over the world; it is a major exporter of capital. All this progress arouses my great admiration, especially as God has endowed the island with few natural resources — no oil or gas and few minerals. It has to import nearly all the raw materials it needs to produce finished goods. The key has been the hard work, inventiveness and ingenuity of its people. This transformation Has been achieved without shedding blood or military coups, only plenty of verbal abuse and some fist-fighting in the Legislative Yuan (parliament).

Most impressive to me has been the explosion of civil society after the end of martial law in July 1987; it was one of the last major decisions taken by President Chiang Ching-kuo who knew he did not have long to live. Freed from the constraints of martial law, religious, civic, academic, professional and community groups burst into action. Today, they organise all kinds of activities, in sports, education, charity, arts, music, culture, publishing and other fields. They have greatly enriched the lives of Taiwan people, giving them choice and diversity they did not have before.

Over the last 40 years, it has been an honour to have walked this journey together with so many Taiwan people. I am not knowledgeable nor qualified enough to write a comprehensive history of Taiwan. But I hope my own personal journey reflected in these pages will help the reader understand one of the most remarkable transformations in the world.

1

MARTIAL LAW

It was early one morning in the summer of 1981. I was asleep in the apartment of a friend in the city of Hsinchu, in northwest Taiwan; it was my first night in this new land. I was awakened by a chorus of male voices coming through the open window. I crawled out of bed and peered out; below was the sports field of a military camp. Jogging around it were twenty soldiers, crew cut in white t-shirts and khaki shorts, singing an army song. On a pole at the top of the field flew a flag of a white sun over a blue sky and the red earth—the flag of the Republic of China. The sun had not yet risen, it was the gray light of dawn. "We all have to do that," said my host, Wang Li, who had walked into the room. "Two years of military service is compulsory for men in Taiwan. I used to do that jogging every morning before breakfast, whatever the weather. We are living under martial law, remember." Wang's apartment was modest, similar to those I had seen in Hong Kong; it had two bedrooms, a sitting room where the family took their meals, kitchen and bathroom. It turned out to be typical of those in urban Taiwan.

The sight of the singing conscripts was a good introduction to a newcomer to Taiwan—or the Republic of China on Taiwan, as it is officially called. After two and a half fascinating years as a reporter and newsreader at Radio Hong Kong, I needed to improve my very limited skillset. I had some understanding of Cantonese, the language most widely used in Hong Kong. Learning Mandarin, the national language of Taiwan and of the People's Republic on the Mainland, would, I thought, be a good step forward. I had met Wang Li, a graduate student, in Hong Kong. He told me Taiwan had excellent language schools and many foreign students. He very kindly invited me to stay with him and his family for the first week of my stay — leading the blind man through the forest.

Wang was kind enough to show me around his home city. It is on the northwest coast of Taiwan, sixty-five kilometers southwest of the capital, Taipei. We walked through streets narrow and crowded with food stalls, restaurants and shops piled high with goods. Wang told me most of the goods were made in Taiwan; it had become a big producer of consumer goods, mostly for export. The streets were full of motorcycles laden with goods and people; they were noisy and crowded. He pointed out a stall selling betel nuts; these are areca nuts chewed with slaked lime and betel leaves as a stimulant and narcotic. I had seen them widely consumed in India; one evening a wealthy man in Madras (now Chennai) invited me to a long dinner. After we had finished the food, he rang a bell to summon his servant. Foolishly still thinking like a European, I was expecting coffee, brandy and cigars — but the servant brought a gold-colored tray with a variety of betel nuts. My host picked up a leaf and carefully chose the nuts to put inside it. He made one leaf for himself and one for me; it was impolite to refuse. The taste was bitter and peppery — my first and last experience of betel nut. Wang told me that chewing the nuts was popular with lorry drivers, factory workers and farm laborers — people with long, repetitive jobs. On the street, I often saw pools of red; initially, I thought it was a result of a fist or gunfight — then remembered it was a lover of betel nut clearing his mouth.

Wang was attending the National Tsing Hua University (NTHU), one of six universities in Hsinchu. What was its relation to the one with the same name in Beijing, I asked. He explained that, after the defeat of the Nationalist government in 1949, the president of NTHU and members of his faculty had come to Taiwan with the retreating government. In 1956, they re-established NTHU in Hsinchu. Later, I discovered the same thing had happened to many institutions. They were re-founded in Taiwan with the same or similar name to the original one in the Mainland. It was confusing; I wondered how many letters and parcels intended for an institution in Taiwan arrived at the twin in the Mainland or vice versa; or passengers for Beijing who took China Airlines and found themselves in Taipei instead. Wang said that, in addition to the universities, the pride of Hsinchu was its Science Park, set up in December 1980 and modeled on Silicon Valley in California. The government wanted a science and technology park to make products more valuable than the bicycles, sports shoes, televisions and other consumer goods that were the main exports at the time. We will learn more about the park later in this story. But suffice it to say that this was probably the single best economic decision taken by the government after its arrival in 1949. The park has given birth to more than four hundred high-tech companies; today it is the largest single source of economic growth on the island. The most famous is Taiwan Semiconductor Manufacturing Company (TSMC), founded in 1987. By 2022, it had become the largest dedicated semi-conductor foundry in the world, with revenues that year of NT$2,263.89 billion ($74.2 billion), an increase of 42.6 per cent compared with 2021, and operations around the world. Wang was polite and well-educated; I felt he wanted to show the best face of Taiwan to the visitor.

After his warm welcome, he kindly put me on the train for Taipei, the best place to study Mandarin. I aimed to cover the cost of the lessons by earning money through journalism, editing and/or teaching. Since Taipei was the capital, it was the best location to find such work. The first thing was to find a place to live. On the advice of friends, I went to the International House of Taipei (IHT), a three-story building on Hsin Yi Road, one of the city's main thoroughfares, with good bus connections. It was a wide road, with three lanes of traffic in two directions; the dominant mode of traffic was scooters, fast and elusive—when you crossed the road, you had to be on full alert. The scooters carried both people and goods. Founded in 1957, the IHT had forty-one rooms for students and residents, including Taiwan people and foreigners, ideal for a greenhorn like myself who knew almost nobody. The rooms were modest, with a minimum of furniture; nearly all the residents were men. People stayed for between three months and two years. It had a library, reading room, restaurant, and sports hall and tennis courts. It was very clean and, for a building full of young men, quiet. My room on the first floor faced Hsin Yi Lu. It had no air conditioning; so, to escape the intense heat of the summer, I had to go to the library.

"By seven in the morning, it was a mad harum-scarum of trucks, cars and motor cyclists," I wrote in a letter in December 1981. "At 7:30 a.m., army recruits will come jogging past and, if I am lucky, a huge red American gas-guzzler with police outriders that is used by the President. On schooldays, the early morning is full of schoolchildren, the boys with crew cuts and the girls also with a uniform hair style in line with the bottom of the ear. Long hair is very rare in Taiwan, so I feel uncomfortable with anything but a short hairdo."

I bought a bicycle—it became my principal form of transport in the city. Work on the Taipei Metro did not begin until 1988; it opened in 1996. The main challenge on the streets was to avoid the mad taxi drivers and "the Evel Knievels on their Suzukis", as I called them. My main sports were jogging, table tennis and basketball; football, my first choice, was hard to find. The two most popular sports in Taiwan were basketball and baseball, a legacy of its Japanese and American heritage. Since I was taller than most Taiwanese, friends invited me to join their basketball game. But, when they saw how little I found the net, they regretted their choice.

The next task was to find a school. Since 1949, Taiwan had been the world center for the study of Mandarin. It could have been mainland China, but when he came to power in 1949, Chairman Mao Zedong expelled almost all the foreigners. The only ones who remained were a small number of 'fellow travelers', those sympathetic to the communist cause who were allowed to stay. They worked as teachers, technical advisers, journalists, editors and in other professions. In the 1950s, about 10,000 Soviet specialists also came to work on big industrial projects. Then, in the early 1960s, they too were expelled after the Sino-Soviet split over ideology. From 1966 to 1976, China fell into the chaos and destruction of the Cultural Revolution that lasted until the death of Mao in September 1976.

So, for more than thirty years after 1949, most of those wanting to learn Mandarin went to study in Taiwan. They included not only Europeans and Americans, Koreans and Japanese, but also thousands of so-called Overseas Chinese, that is people of Chinese ancestry, especially from Southeast Asia. They lived in countries that had restricted or banned Chinese-language education; the governments feared such schools might become a breeding ground for the revolution that Mao wanted to export. At home, most overseas Chinese used Cantonese, Fujianese, Chaozhou or other dialects of their parents' ancestral place; in the 19th and first half of the 20th centuries, few Chinese migrants came from Mandarin-speaking areas. The parents of these children wanted them to learn the national language. Due to this constant flow of students over three decades, I was spoiled for choice. I could select several public or private universities or institutions that offered Mandarin.

I asked teachers and other foreign students for advice. In the end, I chose the Taipei Language Institute (TLI), a private school established in 1956; it was a walk of ten minutes from IHT. The main attraction of TLI was that it offered specialized classes in which students could choose the subject matter. Over age thirty, I felt old; most foreign students were in their twenties. I needed to concentrate on learning the Chinese of journalism and economics, my career, and did not have the luxury of time to learn the vocabulary of other subjects not related to my work.

The class numbers were smaller and fees higher than in public universities, including one-on-one classes; I thought it a good investment. It had a branch with classrooms on the fourth floor of a modern office building in downtown Taipei, easy to reach from IHT. Comfortable and air conditioned, it was a good place to study. The first weeks were instructive. Three of my fellow students were American missionaries; they came to learn not Mandarin, but Taiwanese, the Chinese variant language spoken by a majority of the population which was almost identical to the language spoken in the Fujian port city of Xiamen. They planned, after graduation, to live in central and southern Taiwan and evangelize people using the language. Everyone else wanted to learn Mandarin, to help them in business or academic study, or simply to try something different to what they had done before.

The teachers informed us that we would learn the traditional characters used there, in Hong Kong and Macau and in most Overseas Chinese communities, not the simplified ones adopted by the Mainland in 1958. The change was aimed largely at combatting illiteracy that stood at 80 percent of the population in the early 1950s. Our teachers expressed strong feelings over this and said the simplified characters were "not standard". In being simplified, many had lost their design and meaning, they said. For example, the character for 'love' (*ai*) was 愛 in the traditional form, but in simplified form 爱 – the character had lost 心, 'xin', the heart. To character for fly (*fei*), in traditional form is 飛, with two "wings", but the simplified form 飞 has only one wing. The teachers forbade us from writing simplified characters; only traditional ones were acceptable in class and for homework.

From the depth of their emotions, I came to realize their opinion was not simply a matter of professional judgment, but something more personal. All our teachers were from families that had escaped to Taiwan in 1949 with President Chiang Kai-shek and his government. He brought with him about 1.5 million people, including soldiers, civil servants, business people and intellectuals. We called them 'Mainlanders'. The other residents were Taiwanese, who numbered six million; their forebears had arrived from China, mostly from Fujian Province in the 19th century. Our teachers expressed sadness and bitterness at being forced to leave their homes, lives and families in Beijing, Shanghai, Nanjing and other cities. They were full of anger against everything in the Mainland.

In 1958, the Beijing government introduced a second major reform in addition to the simplified characters. This was pinyin, a way to transliterate Chinese words using letter from the Western alphabet. Students at primary school in the Mainland tend to learn pinyin before they learn characters and simple school textbooks carry the pinyin pronunciation above the characters, enabling students to read them. Taiwan schools used a different older system called Bopomofo, based on ancient characters, which they also learned before the characters. So what should we foreigners learn? For westerners, pinyin would have been the easiest but, since that was from the Mainland, it was out of the question. Learning Bopomofo would have been difficult and time-consuming so our teachers told us to learn the characters directly. They gave us a certain number to learn each week. "Do not spend every night at the bar or the disco," they said. "Go to your room and write the characters repeatedly until you remember them." Perhaps I was fortunate. I felt a measure of desperation in needing to learn. I had spent too many years studying subjects of little use—ten years of both Latin and classical Greek—and could not waste more time. This came home to me most vividly in my teenage years when our Greek teacher took our class on our first study trip in Athens. I prepared a short arrival speech. When we reached the airport immigration desk, I told the officer how happy we were to be in his country and that its illustrious history had taught so much to us fellow Europeans. He shook his head and summoned his superior. I repeated the speech— the same incomprehension. I turned to our teacher and asked if I had mispronounced the words. "No," he said. "But you are talking ancient, not modern, Greek. They cannot understand." We envied our brothers and sisters in Holland, Germany and the Nordic countries who were busy learning the modern languages of Europe; they used them in their daily and business lives.

We foreigners had many things to help us in our studies. The Taiwan students in IHT were polite and helpful in responding to our troublesome questions. We were surrounded by characters, on the bus, street signs, the newspapers and television. We eagerly looked for ones we had learned. In addition, the school kindly helped us to arrange language exchanges—one hour of English and one hour of Chinese. I had several of these each month—they cost nothing, other than the tea, coffee or beer, and it was an excellent way to learn of the life, family and history of Taiwan people. Such personal relations would have been impossible in Mainland China at that time.

This is from a letter I wrote to a friend in England in July 1982: "I am as happy as Wittgenstein in my bare room, with hard bed and wooden chair, gallons of green tea and the army of scooters outside my window. I am trying hard not to make friends and to keep my eyes to the floor (studying). I had my hair cut like a Taiwanese today; food consumption must be the next area for purge."

I remember especially two fellow residents of IHT. One was an extremely thin Englishman in his 50s. His room was spotless; every pencil and spoon was in its proper place. He invited me for tea and biscuits, but never too many. Daunted by the gap in age and experience, I did not feel I could ask too much about his life. He had lived in Taipei for several years; he earned his living teaching English, not in language schools, but to members of the elite, like deputies of the Parliament and business executives, one to one. One student, he said, was in his eighties and went swimming every morning. He would have earned a comfortable living from this. I had no sense of his family or marital status.

The other was Peter, a Swiss-German, far more advanced in Mandarin than I but closer in age, so conversation was easier. He was writing a doctorate in Chinese comparing Machiavelli to a Chinese philosopher of similar mind called Han Fei-zi, who lived in the 4th Century BC; Mao Zedong was greatly influenced by him. Peter had done translation work from Chinese and English and vice versa for the government; both were foreign languages to him. Peter was engaged to a Taiwan lady who worked in the computer section of one of the biggest textile firms; they planned to settle in Switzerland. Peter used to visit the German club in Taipei.

One member was Chiang Wei-kuo, brother of President Chiang Ching-kuo and a retired Army General. He was born in Tokyo, son of a Chinese journalist and senior member of the Kuomintang, and a Japanese lady; Chiang Kai-shek adopted him as his second son. He sent him to a military academy in Munich in Nazi Germany; he joined the Wehrmacht and commanded a Panzer unit during the invasion of Austria. His unit was about to enter Poland, when his father recalled him to China to join the war effort against Japan. Peter told me that Wei-kuo spoke fluent German. "People would ask him to do the Nazi goose-step. Initially, he would decline. But, after a few beers, he would agree. Then we saw how it really was." Later Peter earned a master's from National Taiwan University—no small feat for a foreigner writing a thesis in Chinese on a complex historical topic.

Taiwan was under martial law. There were police stations everywhere; Taipei was very safe. Late one evening in July 1981, I went for a walk downtown with Maurice, a British fellow resident of the IHT. He had come directly from Britain to study Mandarin, for a change of scene and ambience; he did not have a specific objective. We were walking along an ill-lighted pavement outside the main city government office; we were discussing whether Maurice had better marriage prospects with a Korean or French Indian woman in his Mandarin class. I felt a sharp pain in my back and turned to see two terrified Chinese faces; the two men took off at high speed. I looked down and saw blood pouring down Maurice's leg. We hobbled to a nearby police station. As we entered, I saw my trousers were caked in blood too.

Alarmed to see two foreigners attacked in the city center, the officers summoned a taxi. One joined us and stayed with us on the short ride to a hospital. Staff put us face down on a bed and doctor gave each of us four stitches. "You are a lucky boy," a nurse said. "If the knife had gone an inch further, it would have punctured the kidney and you would be in another place." Both Maurice and I had been stabbed in the back with a knife. My wounds were six centimeters deep in the lower left back and nine centimeters in the left buttock. Maurice had two, both six centimeters, in the left buttock. After injections and stitching, I felt more comfortable. We were in a large ward full of family members visiting their loved ones. Many came to see this spectacle of two Big-Noses lying face down and were asking how this had come about.

The doctor told us that, after we returned home, we must remain lying down for four weeks to allow the wounds to heal. Later that night, we returned to IHT. The Taiwan students were stunned. They expected such violence in downtown New York, Chicago or Johannesburg but not in martial-law Taipei. Out of shame, they became very solicitous. Maurice and I had visitors throughout the day, bringing tea, coffee, cakes, sweets and comfort. We were in no state to investigate what had happened. The students said we were walking near New Park, a well-known pick-up point for gay men. The attackers may have thought we were on our way there; many Chinese detested homosexuality and considered it a disease imported by Westerners. We never had official confirmation of this.

This is what I wrote about the episode in a letter to a friend: "It took about two months in all to heal, and the first weeks I was extremely nervous. This country is under martial law, and unexplained things happen from time to time. Government control is strict, mail and phones are censored. For a month, I was uneasy. But, when I went back to Hong Kong to renew the visa, it was as quick as normal, so I figured there was nothing to worry about." I was touched by the care and concern of the Taiwan students, and had suffered no lasting injury. So I decided to stay on. After two newspapers carried the story, Maurice and I gained a little prominence.

When I went to the international airport a few weeks later to go to Hong Kong to renew the visa, many people came forward and said words like, "I'm sorry this happened to you. It is a disgrace to the nation." In a letter I wrote at that time: "Is this not civility and fine manners? Would a Chinese mugged in New York or London have the same reaction?" Maurice was so shaken by the stabbing he decided to end his studies in Taipei; he returned to the UK two months later.

To earn money to cover the cost of classes and living expenses, the best option was to write freelance articles for media clients outside Taiwan. But, at the start, my Chinese was too poor and knowledge of the island too limited for this. In addition, interest in the outside world in Taiwan was limited. After thirty years of self-imposed isolation, Mainland China was opening to the world; that is what foreign editors wanted to know about. So I needed to look elsewhere. A friend introduced a position at the United Daily News (UDN), one of Taiwan's two big newspapers, founded in 1951. Under martial law, the media had to support the ruling Kuomintang.

The UDN had a weekly English-language magazine, China Economic News (CEN), which needed an editor, to work each afternoon and Saturday morning. It paid NT$19,500 for a twenty-three-hour week, enough to cover class and living expenses. Perfect—language classes in the morning, editing in the afternoon. UDN had a large office building across town; it was a pleasant twenty-five-minute bicycle ride. The CEN office was on the sixth floor, in a large room of journalists and editors; the editor and reporters were Taiwanese, helped by a small number of expatriates to improve the copy and to offer opinions. It was a large, open office; the editor could see what everyone was doing. Since it was on the sixth floor, there was plenty of sunlight. During the hot sultry summers, air conditioning was essential.

That first afternoon was the start of my education about Taiwan's economy. The editor, a retired Army Major named Osman, took me to a side room to explain the rules. "China is the Republic of China, you understand," he said. "China's Ministry of Foreign Affairs is the one here. If you have to mention the one in the Mainland, you must use quotation marks around his title and add "Communist China". The legal government of China is here and the one in the Mainland is not legal, you understand. The name of the country is Republic of China. Do not refer to Taiwan as a country."

In references to President Chiang Ching-kuo, his late father Chiang Kai-shek and other members of his family, we had to be very careful and use only official titles and descriptions. We were forbidden to criticize the political leaders or national policy 'to recover the Mainland'.

"Do not use the word 'Taiwanese' nor refer to the 'Taiwanese' language," Osman said.

I asked why. "There is tension between the Mainlanders who came here with President Chiang in 1949 and those already here. The subject is sensitive and we must not refer to it. Call people 'citizens of the RoC'. There are other things you need to know. We will tell you over the coming weeks." The UDN had a locked room — accessible to only four people — which contained communist newspapers from the Mainland and Hong Kong. The four edited stories from the papers and published them in the UDN; it was an easy job because the readers had no other sources of information about the 'other place'. I gradually came to understand the rules and taboos of the CEN and the UDN. Media all over the world have their own rules that their staff must follow. Everyone at CEN was polite and friendly; as time passed, I understood more.

One evening Osman took me out for a drink. "You know how I ended up here?" he said. "I was born in a village in Hubei in Central China. In 1948, I was fourteen and playing in the street when the Nationalist army arrived. It was short of recruits (for the war with the communists) and forced me and other young men to join. We could not even say goodbye to our families. So I became a soldier and arrived to Taiwan in 1949, like thousands of others."

"How is your English so good?" I asked.

"I had a two-year posting in Quemoy."

This is an island, also known as Jinmen, held by the RoC that is swimming distance from Fujian Province held by the People's Republic; it is the front line. "When we were not on duty, we lived in underground dormitories and rooms. After dinner, I used a torchlight to read English books and learn the language. It gave me something useful to do." After he left the army, he went into journalism.

Our most charismatic reporter was Wendell Chang. Handsome, he was well dressed and was said to have many girlfriends. He was a native of Taiwan; he served in the army not as a professional soldier like Osman but doing his two years of compulsory service.

"I was based on Quemoy. Night duty was frightening," he told me. "There was blackout on the island each day after 1900. Three colleagues and I patrolled the beaches facing Xiamen (in Mainland China). It was pitch black, with the only light from the moon, the stars and our torches. Each side sent frogmen across the narrow strait of water during the night to murder soldiers of the other and return before dawn. In the early hours of one morning we entered a military hut on the beach. Inside, we found four of our men stabbed to death. On the wall was written in blood, 'They were sleeping.' The PLA men had used knives, not guns, so as not to attract attention. When you were not patrolling, you lived underground, in a huge network of tunnels."

The job at CEN was ideal—twenty-three hours a week and not too demanding. Dress code was conservative—white shirt and dark trousers. We wore a tie when there was an important meeting. The men had short hair, the women kept theirs neat and tied up. It had a military feel. My Chinese colleagues, and the small number of foreigners, were very helpful. I was able to learn much from the stories I had to edit and the journalists who wrote them. It made a pleasant change from staring at rows of characters, which we had to write down and memorize. I gradually understood the 'parallel universe' created by the RoC government in Taiwan. One slogan painted on many streets was " 光復大陸" ("Guangfu Dalu", meaning "Recover the Mainland"). I took this to mean that, at the appropriate time, the government planned to invade China and resume control of it.

We were in 1981, thirty-two years since the Kuomintang government arrived in Taiwan. When would the invasion happen? One of the editors in our office was a good person to ask—Kenneth Liu, son of a senior officer in the KMT Air Force. In a bar, I asked him.

"Sorry, I cannot answer you. It is a military secret," he replied. We chatted about other topics; a few beers later, I asked him again.

"You foreigners laugh at us and say we will not do it. But I tell you that we will. It is a question of time." We downed more glasses and became more blurred.

Then Kenneth said, "What I can tell you is that the invasion date is getting closer. Maybe even next year." That would be 1982. Not sure if the army changed its plan, or something unexpected happened; in any event, an invasion did not happen that year.

United Daily News was one of the two biggest newspapers in Taiwan. It was rich and celebrated its 30th anniversary in 1981, in the spacious building where we worked. To mark the event, they gave all the staff a wrist watch, a box of special cakes; a tie and a cake on the staff member's birthday. After work, I often went to the office canteen, for which we were given free meal tickets. The salary covered the IHT rent and tuition, plus food and consumer goods, which were cheaper than in Hong Kong, leaving a little to spare.

Staying in the IHT and working at the magazine, I was invited to enjoyable parties at the weekends. As befitting a society under martial law and in which adult males had to serve in the military, the atmosphere was more conservative than parties in Hong Kong and Europe—beer and wine, yes, but no drugs. Most of the participants dressed in a conservative fashion, especially the ladies; many did not drink alcohol. The number of foreigners in Taiwan was not high, so we Big-Noses were the object of curiosity. Americans accounted for the largest non-Chinese group in Taiwan.

The main questions at parties were: "what are you doing here? How long do you plan to stay? What do you think of our country?" After attending several of these events, I noticed American men received special attention from the ladies.

At one, a pretty lady asked me where I was from. "Britain," I replied. "To which state of the US does that belong?" she asked.

To which I responded, "In the future, it may become a state, but at the moment it is independent." Without saying a word, the lady turned away; she did not want to waste a moment more talking to such a person. Puzzled, I asked a foreign student at IHT who had lived in Taiwan for three years to explain. "If a Taiwan person has a place at a foreign university and sufficient funding, he or she can obtain a passport and exit visa," he said. "If not, it is not easy to leave the country. Marrying a foreigner is the easiest way, and the United States is the most desirable destination. As a result, single American men are very popular here." Indeed, they were. But I often wondered if the Americans, especially the new arrivals, realized the reason for their popularity. Some mistook the attention they received from attractive young ladies for admiration for their physique, charm and intellect.

This is what I wrote in a letter in October 1981: "the contrast between American and Chinese students is startling. With a few exceptions, the Americans are easy-going about their studies — they give Mandarin a try. Well, if they do not like it, they can always study Hindi, law or perhaps sub-aqua [scuba-diving]. They can all earn NT\$250-300 an hour for teaching English, double the top rate for studying Mandarin. Their wealth gives them, I think, too many choices, so they can never fix on one for longer than six months. The Chinese students, from Hong Kong or Taiwan, are the opposite. They have access to limited financial resources and competition both here and to get to the US is intense, so they study very hard, complain rarely and never change course. I learned this week that Taiwan has more people per head attending post-secondary education than Britain. This is a truly astonishing statistic. Britain has far more universities than Taiwan — but folks here catch up by attending night school in huge numbers."

Needing a good Chinese-English dictionary, I asked a fellow student in IHT where to buy one. "Go to the underpass leading to Taipei railway station and you will find a good selection," he said.

"Not a bookshop?" I asked.

He laughed. "Taiwan is the kingdom of fakes. You can find there excellent items for a bargain price," he said. Following his advice, I went to the underpass. He was right. Stalls there sold high-quality counterfeit goods. Among them was a large dictionary by Lin Yu-tang, one of the most famous Chinese authors and translators of the 20th Century, with good paper and binding. The price of $12 showed that it was fake. I bought it and used it for the rest of my time in Taiwan.

"How about a Rolex watch?" the lady asked. I did not buy one that day but did several weeks later, for $21. They became the gifts I presented to relatives at home during the annual summer visit. They were a big hit. One cousin liked to sit at the bar in his local pub with his arm upright, so the other patrons could see and admire it. They took it as a sign of how smart and wealthy he was — although his clothes suggested the contrary. It had the same good outcome for me; family members believed I had done much better in the mysterious Orient than other evidence suggested. This magic worked for three years. Then, unfortunately, the British media began to publish stories on the skill and ingenuity of the Taiwan counterfeiters. That summer I presented a Rolex to a family friend.

"This is a fake you are giving me?" he said angrily. "What kind of gift is that?" After that, I had no choice but to switch to more expensive items.

During the early 1980s, the counterfeiters made all kinds of products, including computers, Nike and Adidas sportswear, brand clothes and Snoopy dolls. The American companies that owned the brands worked aggressively against them; they hired private investigators and worked with the police to conduct raids. Since Taiwan depended on the US for its defense and a major export market, the government had no alternative but to cooperate. During the 1980s, the island's manufacturers moved up the economic ladder and no longer needed to rely on counterfeits. The police moved against those who sold fakes and the production moved to Mainland China and Southeast Asia. You could still find the fakes, but it was troublesome. First, you had to convince the dealer that you were not an agent of the U.S. government or manufacturer; then he gave you the address of a nearby street and told you to go to the third floor. Knock on the locked door, more questions and, if you were lucky, you could buy the item. The American pressure worked.

Taiwan imposed import tariffs on many goods. This offered an opportunity to those traveling to and from Hong Kong—a duty-free port—to make a little money. The business was well organized. I and others went to a designated shop in Hong Kong and bought the maximum amount of cigarettes, liquor and other items that Taiwan allowed travelers to bring in without duty. After arrival in Taipei, we took them to the partner travel agent who gave us double the price. The difference usually covered the cost of the air ticket. The travel agent then sold the goods to Taiwan people and made a profit.

2

CROSS-STRAIT FLIGHT

It was a quiet afternoon in November 1983. In the newspaper office, we were busy editing articles about Taiwan exports of electronic components and the need to move up the technology ladder away from badminton rackets and rubber shoes. Suddenly, deputy editor Kenneth announced dramatically, "Everyone, stop working. Watch the television." It was transmitting live coverage from Chiang Kai-shek International Airport southwest of Taipei of what the newspapers called "a flight to freedom". Wang Xue-cheng, a pilot in the People's Liberation Army, had just arrived there, having flown his MiG-19 jet fighter 700 kilometres from his base in the Zhoushan Islands, southeast of Shanghai. We watched images of the plane, with its PLA markings, surrounded by uniformed members of the Taiwan military and delighted officials.

Two cleaning ladies arrived in the office with trolleys of beer. Everyone was handed a bottle and invited to start drinking; there was soon a party atmosphere. People left their desks, watched the television and started chatting. The reporter at the airport described how the Taiwan Air Force had picked up the MiG on its radar screens and scrambled fighters to intercept it. Wang deployed his landing gear and rocked his wings to show that he wanted to land. The fighters escorted him down to the airport to land. After getting out of the plane, he told officials that he wanted to surrender. The Taiwan government had a standing offer to PLA pilots who arrived with a MiG-19; it gave Wang 3,000 taels of gold. The reporter said that Wang was the seventh pilot to have defected from China since 1949; three had gone to South Korea and four had come to Taiwan. Delighted to have the afternoon off, everyone gathered around the television and exchanged stories. For the government, the defection was proof of the 'superiority' of its system — just as it was hailed when Taiwan pilots flew the other way.

I asked Kenneth what he thought. Since his father was in the Air Force, he would know what was going on.

"Of course, we are happy about this. We can thoroughly examine the MiG-19 and that will help improve our defenses," he said. "But do not believe all you see. Wang will be very well received, will be given a large sum of money, a nice apartment and a new wife. He will have an office job but will never be allowed to fly a plane again. It is too dangerous. Can we really trust him?" Later Wang was given the rank of major in the Taiwan Air Force and divorced his Chinese wife. He married a Taiwan lady; they had a son and two daughters. But he maintained contact with his family in Henan Province on the Mainland and called them regularly by telephone. In August 1983, another PLA pilot, Sun Tianqin, had also defected, to South Korea and from there, he came to Taiwan. In January 1985, he married a Chinese musician who had defected to Taiwan. After Sun left the Taiwan Air Force, the two emigrated to Canada.

The defection and the celebrations that followed were a vivid illustration of the dreadful relations between the two sides, even thirty-four years after the civil war had ended on the Mainland. During those three decades, the Taiwan economy had made great advances; its people had become richer, better educated and more worldly. But, in politics, the two faced each other with unswerving hostility. There were no direct air, sea or postal links between them; only birds could fly between the two places. People and goods going from one to the other had to transit through a third place—Hong Kong, Okinawa, Japan or South Korea.

This was especially hard on the tens of thousands of families split by the civil war. I discovered that the case of Osman, press-ganged into the Nationalist army without saying goodbye to his family, was common. Soldiers, civil servants, business people and many others had come to Taiwan on their own and left members of their family behind. The husband—often a soldier—came, leaving his wife and children. As the two sides settled into their deep hostility, sending letters or parcels or making telephone calls became increasingly difficult; each was looking for spies from the other side. Most people gave up hope of reuniting with their Mainland family and formed a new one in Taiwan. One of our teachers at TLI did that. A native of Beijing, he arrived in Taiwan in 1949 on his own, without his wife. Unable to bring her over, he divorced her and married a Taiwan lady. Everyone was careful what they said and wrote.

One day, I was walking along a Taipei street looking for a postbox; I found one and was about to post the letter, when a man rushed forward.

"No, do not post it there. Use the red one down the street," he said pointing thirty meters ahead.

"Is this not a postbox?" I asked.

"No, this is for information on communist agents," he said. It was my mistake; I had not read the characters correctly. If you suspected a colleague or neighbor was such an agent, you were supposed to report him or her through these boxes.

Another day I was traveling in a bus along a long road

close to the Tamsui River that runs through Taipei. It stopped at a traffic light. Suddenly, ten soldiers with weapons appeared out of a manhole and ran fifty meters along the road; then they disappeared into another manhole. I assumed that, in the event of an attack by the PLA, the army had built tunnels underground to take shelter. In 1965, President Chiang opened the National Palace Museum in Taipei, to house the art treasures he had brought from the Forbidden City in Beijing. He chose a mountain north of the city and built the museum and the storerooms in the side of the mountain. It was the same logic. If there was an air attack, the museum above ground might be hit — but the pieces kept inside the mountain would be safe.

In December 1981, I had the good fortune to meet Helmut, an Austrian who worked as a journalist for his country's national radio station in Beijing. He was in Taiwan to do a story on the island. He described a news conference in Beijing by a Taiwan pilot who had defected there in August 1981. "He said he had done so because he disagreed with the RoC government's hardline refusal to negotiate towards a united China," Helmut explained. "We were all skeptical (of this explanation). Rumors circulated that he did it either because of gambling debts of NT$1 million — NT$3 million or a failed love affair.

The pilot said he flew his aircraft directly into Chinese airspace, but his co-pilot said he did not want to defect. So they flew back over an RoC offshore island, where the pilot ejected. Then he flew back again. He expected to meet Chinese fighters but there were none, no defense system of any kind. He had to look for an airport and, when he found one, he landed there. No one noticed him except for some workmen repairing the runway. He received a big reward of course." Two years later, we heard a rumor about the defector — he had married an airline hostess but took his own life because he could find nothing to spend his fortune on and was completely bored. And the co-pilot who ejected was given a seven-year prison sentence for not shooting him — his best friend. As with most news about the military, we could not confirm this.

The front line of the conflict between the two sides was the island of Quemoy, also known as Jinmen or Kinmen. Geographically, it was part of Fujian Province, but, after 1949, it was held by the Taiwan military. It is just ten kilometers from the Mainland city of Xiamen and within easy shelling distance. It was the site of intense battles in 1949 and 1950 and during two crises in the Taiwan Strait in the 1950s. After 1958, the two sides settled into a routine of bombarding each other on alternate days with shells containing propaganda leaflets. This continued for twenty years. For Taiwan army conscripts like my CEN colleagues, an assignment to Quemoy was the most feared and dangerous, as Wendell Chang describes in the last chapter. Access to the island was severely restricted, especially for foreigners.

I heard a first-hand account of the island in May 1982. Friend Hugh Sandeman, the Economist bureau chief in Tokyo, arrived for a two-week reporting trip. With half of the magazine's circulation in the US, the Government Information Office gave him red-carpet treatment, including interviews with the Ministers of Economics and Finance and the deputy secretary-general of the KMT, one of the top strategic advisers to the President. They also flew him in an ageing military plane — he was the sole passenger — for the eighty-minute journey to Quemoy.

This is how he described it: "a showcase island, a fortress underneath. We were taken down underground tunnels and shown rows of tanks, a huge hospital and a huge cinema, which is the people's main recreation. There was a pill-box at every crossroad. When I asked the colonel what the men did about the lack of women, he said that was classified. I was shown an enormous loudspeaker built into a thirty-five foot-high block of concrete, which blasted propaganda to the other side. They keep no aircraft on the island because they would be too vulnerable. If the rest of Taiwan is less doctrinaire than I thought it would be, Quemoy is not. It has to be that way. Otherwise how can they keep the morale of the soldiers up? And their political stance leaves them no choice but to continue keeping so many men there." When the soldiers were not on patrol or exercises above the ground, they spent their time in these rooms and tunnels underground. That was the price they paid for the Cold War.

Later, friends told me that the Taiwan military did provide ladies to meet the needs of its soldiers on Quemoy. One even said women criminals who were about to be sent to jail were offered a greatly reduced sentence if they agreed to 'serve' in Quemoy for a limited period. None of this was confirmed by the army at the time. But, after the end of martial law in July 1987, they did. The island was handed over to civil administration in the 1990s; they developed it as a tourist destination for Taiwan and mainland people. You can visit where the brothels used to be; now they have become tourist attractions. A film was made about them. You can also buy vegetable knives made out of the thousands of shells fired there by the People's Liberation Army.

One of my conversation partners was a student named Edward Wang. He was intelligent, sophisticated and destined for a successful career in the government. He dressed smartly and liked to meet in an old-style tea shop. We did things in the traditional way — washing the cups with hot water and throwing away the first cup. He belonged to the Kuomintang elite. His family had come from the Mainland in 1949; his father was an army doctor, giving him excellent credentials. He was studying at the National Chengchi (Politics) University and planned to earn a PhD in the United States and join the Foreign Ministry. I asked him if that was really the best choice. In 1971, China had replaced Taiwan at the United Nations; in 1979, Washington had cut ties with Taipei to recognize Beijing. Other countries followed suit; a Taiwan diplomat would have increasingly fewer countries to serve in.

I said, "Why not go into an economic ministry and deal with the world that way? You will have more freedom and ability to do things." But he was determined to go for the Foreign Ministry. He was patriotic.

One day he arrived looking much shaken. I asked what had happened.

"I was summoned for a meeting with officers of the Taiwan Garrison Command (TGC)." This was the secret police of which everyone was terrified. In charge of implementing martial law, it was the most powerful security agency on the island. "They said I would soon be going to the US to study for my PhD. When I was there, I should watch over other Taiwan students and report on them to the TGC. They said, 'If you want your career to advance, you will cooperate with us. We will give you a few days to consider your decision'." He said that, in principle, he did not want to spy on his fellow students but was afraid of the consequences if he did not. Could the TGC veto his application for the Foreign Ministry?

I suggested he agree and then write reports with anodyne information—what the students studied, who their girlfriends were and which NBA teams they supported. "If they ask for more information, tell them that you were unable to obtain it," I advised.

In one way, it was a compliment that the TGC approached him. It showed they considered him 'reliable', a member of the ruling elite. The main targets of the TGC were communist agents and those campaigning for democracy, an end to one-party rule and independence. Since campaigning for independence was banned in Taiwan, its leaders lived abroad, in Japan, the United States and elsewhere. On April 24, 1970, Peter Huang, a Taiwan student who supported independence, tried to assassinate Chiang Ching-kuo, then vice-premier, as he was entering the Plaza Hotel in New York. He stepped forward from behind a pillar and was about to fire on Chiang when a security agent knocked his arm upwards and the bullet missed. Huang and his co-conspirator, his brother-in-law, both pleaded guilty but, out on bail, escaped and left the United States.

Edward Wang's father, an army doctor, had spent time in the north of Thailand, caring for members of a Kuomintang army who had escaped from southwest China. While some of its members moved to Taiwan, others remained in Thailand; they helped the Thai government fight a communist insurgency and most were given Thai citizenship. His work in Thailand was part of the ideology of the Republic of China.

My other main conversation partners were three native Taiwanese—Ivan, Henry and Emily. When we met, they were always neat and tidy, with short hair, and dressed conservatively— no long hair or T-shirts with zany slogans. Unlike Edward Wang, they came from ordinary families, had studied hard at school and university and made much of themselves. Ivan's father was a farmer in central Taiwan. After graduation, he went to work for the Taipei office of Mitsubishi Corp, one of the five giant Japanese trading companies; it was a stable, well-paid job even if the top positions were reserved for Japanese. He explained the five Japanese firms controlled a large part of Taiwan's import and export volume. The other four were Mitsui, Itochu, Sumitomo and Marubeni. Ivan spoke warmly about his Japanese bosses.

Later, when I worked in China, I came to realize the power and reach of these firms. When I went to a city outside Beijing, I used to invite the representative of one of them to a lunch. They knew everything about the city, the province and its economy; theirs were worldwide companies that collected information on all areas of life. They were better informed than most governments. So, for a Taiwanese company making textiles, televisions or electronic components, these five were the best choice to sell their goods abroad. Our CEN magazine often ran articles saying these exports should be handled by Taiwan, not Japanese, firms. Everyone knew this change would take time.

At Chinese New Year, Ivan went to stay in the family home in the countryside in central Taiwan. "There men eat separately from the women. Even my wife, a university graduate, has to eat in the kitchen with the other women, while I have dinner with Father and other male relatives. It is insulting for her, but that is how it is. Rural society is more conservative." Ivan had a Spartan lifestyle: he drank boiled water—no tea, coffee or alcohol. On weekends, he went with his wife and friends on long walks in the hills surrounding Taipei. Ivan had come a long way from the poor farm where he grew up in central Taiwan.

"I had seen an airplane, but not a boat or a train until I came to Taipei for the first time at the age of eighteen. My father had no money and no connections and could only offer me the same life as he had. His life was hard and unrewarding. Whatever money he made from selling his produce, the merchant who bought it made more. So the only escape for me was to study." To pass the university exam, he lived for a year in a dormitory in Taipei and attended a cram school. "I was very poor. I used to buy three slices of bread for each meal and spent all the time studying. Some nights I did not go to bed. I just fell asleep on the bench and woke up at 4:00 a.m. and continued. So I passed the exam at the second attempt."

His brother was not so lucky. After graduating from junior

high school, he joined the army for seven years, serving in the artillery. When he left, he had no skills suitable for civilian life; the army arranged a job in the post office for him. In the army, he could not find a wife, so the family found a spouse for him. "He never eats meat before 10:00 a.m. in the morning," Ivan said. "The reason was that he served on Matsu (like Quemoy, an island close to the Mainland). He swore that, if he returned to Taiwan alive, he would, to thank Buddha, be a half-vegetarian."

Henry ran his own small textile company. "Chinese like to run their own businesses and not work for others," he said. "That is why there are so many small and medium-size firms in Taiwan." His family lived in a small apartment in downtown Taipei; his father delivered cylinders for the city gas company. Henry liked to tell jokes. He made fun of the thick Ningbo accent of President Chiang Ching-kuo and his father Chiang Kai-shek.

"When they give a speech on television, few people can understand them—they need subtitles in Chinese," he said. He liked to exchange gossip about members of the Chiang family—something completely banned at the office or in the media. He said two sons of Chiang Ching-kuo liked to drink and party and no one, not even the police or TGC, could control them. "As sons of the 'emperor', they are above the law," Henry said. I suspected many Taipei residents knew this but dared to speak of it only with family or close friends, and never in public.

Emily worked as a secretary in a trading company. She was a pleasant, attractive lady. She often talked about her romantic life. My impression was there was a mismatch in the dating market. Young men had the traditional Chinese idea that a wife should be younger and less educated than they, and obedient. But, due to Taiwan's excellent school system, young women like Emily were as well educated as the men; they had career opportunities not open to their mothers and grandmothers. They wanted an equal relationship with a partner; it was not easy to find one. All three were attending evening classes after their long day in the office—Ivan to learn Japanese, Henry to learn Spanish to help him with his Latin American clients and Emily to learn business management.

Once Emily was absent for three weeks; she needed an operation on her thyroid. When she came back, she had a scar on her neck that was very visible. "You need to give a red packet (with money) to the surgeon before the operation," she said. "Then he will do a better job and there will be no scar. Unfortunately, my family is too poor and could not pay him. This scar will not help me during my dates."

The three rarely talked about politics. They were happy with their lives—they were better educated and better paid than their parents and could look forward to their standard of life improving. This was the social contract offered by the Kuomintang government—no democracy or political reform— but an economy growing every year. It was rightly called an 'economic miracle'. During the 1980s, Taiwan firms moved to making semiconductors and electronic equipment, including radios, television sets and computers. By the mid-1980s, it had become one of the world's largest producers of computers and computer peripherals.

Twenty years later, I went to visit Henry again in Taipei. How well he had done—a large, comfortable house in Tianmu, one of the city's most desirable districts, and a pretty wife younger than he. Henry bought textiles from factories in China. "When I go to the Mainland, I have three rules," he said. "Never wear an expensive watch or designer clothes. They attract attention from potential robbers. Just ready-to-wear suits and a cheap watch, or don't wear a watch at all. And never go to bed with a Mainland lady, however attractive. It is too risky. She may be working for a criminal gang. Its members will catch you in the act, steal your money, credit card and passport and photograph and blackmail you."

Among themselves and at home, Ivan, Henry and Emily spoke Taiwanese. Like me and other foreign students, they had to learn Mandarin at school. After 1945, President Chiang Kai-shek made it the sole official language, in education, the government, the media and the security services in Taiwan. In a school, all the teachers and students might be Taiwanese-speakers, but they had to speak Mandarin even in the playground. One who did not would be scolded and had to wear a board that said, "I must speak Mandarin." By the time I arrived there, the policy had been implemented for more than thirty years, so all those who had been through the school system were comfortable in Mandarin, including Ivan, Henry and Emily.

As an unmarried man in my early 30s and a Big-Nose, I was often invited to parties. I found an ambience more restrained than in Hong Kong or the West, reflecting the conservative society of Taiwan. There was beer and wine, but no drugs. Many women drank sparingly or not at all. They had to be careful of sex before marriage; the pill was available but not so convenient. Some young women did not know where to buy it or were too embarrassed to ask. Nearly all of them wanted to marry and have families. Those with a university education wanted to go on working as well. Parties were an opportunity to meet new people. Taiwan people knew they lived in a greenhouse and wanted to hear news from outside the greenhouse. Foreigners were exotic and more aggressive sexually than Taiwan men; talking to them was also an opportunity to practice English.

The happiest people at these events were the foreign men, especially the Americans, and the least happy the foreign women. This is from a letter I wrote in December 1981 about a Christmas party: "the foreign women stood out, stouter and more poorly dressed than the Chinese girls. I asked one of my Chinese men friends why they seemed out of place. 'I have never been out with a foreign girl,' he replied. 'I do not want to, nor do my friends. In part, this is because we could never marry one. A foreign girl could not get used to living in our way and with our family. For a Chinese girl, it is different. When she marries, she leaves the family anyway and so has more freedom to marry a foreigner. The responsibility of the boy in Taiwan is to support the family. Also I am frightened of foreign women; they are fiercer than Chinese women. They are fatter and I do not find them attractive.' "

One male colleague at CEN said young Taiwan people were too timid: "Chinese girls are taught never to make the first move or show their feelings," he told me. "I was very timid too, so it took two years for us to know each other—even though we were classmates in college and I loved her at first sight" Another colleague said that at his university, the male students did not date the females because they were too bright. "We did not want our role challenged. So the girls at my university went abroad and married there. Their families did not mind, because it is the son who supports the family."

I wrote in a letter in November 1982: "a girl told me the vast majority of her friends would not sleep nor live with a man before marrying him. She herself did not disapprove of the idea but would not do it herself. There were two reasons—one, that there was no commitment and the other that it put her reputation at risk. If it became known, it might ruin her chance of finding the kind of man she liked. I have only met one Chinese girl here who said she does not want children. All the others say they do, though only two or three, rather than the six or seven in their own family.

"Don, a handsome black American student from Harvard, said he did not want to go out with Chinese girls because there were too many complications and they might think you want to marry them. 'In my country, people are very lusty,' he said. 'Everyone knows it, you can see it. But not here, there is nothing to see. The men here seem to have no lust. They are so controlled I cannot believe it. Sex here is only for procreation; in Europe and the US, it is for recreation.' "

The anguish of foreign women was well expressed by Sarah, an American Jewish girl who was in love with Matt, also an American Jew. He was doing what we called 'a timeless dissertation' on a neo-Confucian philosopher. He had never worked in his life but must have received money from somewhere—his US university or rich parents. Blessed—or cursed—by love for Matt, Sarah followed him to Taiwan where he wanted to continue his studies. She was well aware of the risk.

"Why do most foreigners want to study Chinese?" she asked. "They want to find an Asian wife. In the circle in which Matt and I move, we are the only all-white couple. The rest are all mixed. It is a fixation which many whites have. It is the same the other way round. Many Chinese are dying to go out with white women, especially Americans who have the reputation for being the randiest women in the world. I lived once in a dormitory with many Japanese men. They kept asking me, but I did not want to go. They only wanted to go out with me because I was white, not because of myself. I have never found Asian men attractive. Most are not well endowed physically. Look at any bus queue; they are all wearing tight trousers, but there is nothing to see— quite the opposite to American men who have a huge bulge if they wear tight pants. I suspect that white men who run after Asians have the same problem as Asian men—they are sexual weaklings. They want a servant, someone who will obey them, cook for them, wait on them and will not ask any questions. They cannot find women like that anymore in the US, so they have to come to Asia instead." She feared that Matt, for whom she lives, would leave her for a Chinese girl, much like the stereotyped Asian women she described.

At one of these parties, the sister of a colleague whose father was high up in the military told me she despaired of getting married, because there were too many women of her age in Taiwan. This was because, in the 1950s and 1960s, couples would go on having children until they had a son. So there were often several daughters before a son appeared; this accounted for the imbalance. This has changed dramatically. Today Taiwan has one of the lowest birth rates in the world. In 2022, the population in Taiwan shrank for the third consecutive year, falling by 110,674 people from a year earlier; the country saw both its lowest-ever number of births and highest-ever deaths, according to statistics released by the Ministry of the Interior. At the end of 2022, the population stood at 23.265 million, down by 110,674, or 0.47 percent, from a year ago.

One of our teachers, Miss Wang, was elegant and had perfect manners. She had fallen in love with a tall Canadian named Mike who worked for a big American electronics company. He was forty years old and had a car and a three-bedroom apartment, with a big television and VCR machine on which he played films borrowed from the American Club in Taipei. She made the big decision to move in with him. But she kept her own apartment in Taipei, her 'official address' as far as family and friends were concerned. The only member of her family she told was a younger sister to whom she was very close.

Mike was the opposite of the well-brought-up Chinese boy her parents wanted her to marry. He wandered around the flat in the nude, making up to Miss Wang anywhere, with or without company present. His conversation was peppered with references to sex. He had married before but was, he said, in the process of getting a divorce. This secrecy meant Miss Wang could no longer see her old friends or her family except at their home. Her only social circle were Mike's friends, mostly Big-Noses.

Then, by a stroke of bad luck, her mother was reading her sister's diary and found her new telephone number. She called the number—and heard the voice of a male Westerner. So the secret was out. For his part, Mike was not hurrying through his divorce, a common tactic of ex-married people who would rather not be free agents. He asked her if she could consider leaving him, she said, "I could not go back. I have given up everything." The family was polite enough not to oppose the affair publicly. When the couple went to the family home for Chinese New Year, they even gave him the seat of honor. But, in their heart, they were hoping desperately she would leave him. Otherwise, they would lose their beloved daughter across the Pacific.

I saw homosexuality among a few foreigners, but never among Chinese. Since it was a taboo, Chinese gays would not have dared to show their affection in public or at parties attended by people they did not know. We assumed there were some. It was completely beyond our imagination that, just twenty years later, Taipei would in 2003 hold its first gay parade, Taiwan Pride. The event in October 2019 attracted more than 200,000 participants, the largest in Asia and bigger than the Tel Aviv Pride, the largest in the Middle East. In May 2019, the Parliament legalized gay marriage, the first in Asia to do so.

Just before Chinese New Year in 1983, I went to attend the wedding of a friend named Wang Luen. The venue was a restaurant on the fifth floor of a building with many banquet rooms. I stepped out of the lift and was greeted by happy, boisterous people. I presented my wedding present, a red packet with NT$800 ($20) and sat down at the nearest table. A man on my right said he had served in an RAF airbase in Gloucester, England, from 1946-48 — how remarkable. Everyone was welcoming. Then the bride and bridegroom arrived to toast us, as they did each table.

Suddenly, I noticed the bridegroom was not Wang Luen — I had come to the wrong wedding! I excused myself. The people at the table said, "Do not worry, it happens all the time — too many banquets in the same building." I asked the hosts to return the red packet, but they refused. I wandered around the building until I found Mr Wang's wedding. He and his family had a good laugh at the silly foreigner not being able to find the right wedding, even after being in Taiwan for nineteen months. At my request, the restaurant manager was able to retrieve the red packet; I presented it to Mr Wang and his bride. Another wedding I remember had an open table at the front door to greet the guests. Instead of simply handing in your red packet, which was normal, you had also to write your name and the amount you were giving. There was a large sheet of red paper. I looked at the list; the amount, of course, increased with each guest, since you could not give less than others. Fortunately, I was one of the earliest to arrive, so I got away lightly; I only had to add a little to what was in the packet. Pity the latecomers.

One social aspect in which I failed my editors was not drinking. Each Chinese New Year they invited all the staff to a New Year dinner to thank them for their work during the year. The tables were always heaving with food and drink. Osman criticized me for abstaining. Fortunately, he and the others soon became sloshed and did not remember this lapse of manners. The women drank very little and left at about 8:15 p.m., just as the men were just getting into song. This was the pattern for banquets at New Year, other festivals or visits by VIPs. The company also arranged a free annual outing. We jumped on a bus and explored the rice and vegetable fields, hills and mountains and exotic food of towns and villages outside Taipei. These trips were very enjoyable.

Two friends who left a deep impression were a law professor and his wife, who worked in the Taiwan Tobacco & Liquor Company. It was a state monopoly the government inherited from the Japanese when they took over Taiwan in 1945. Both were from the Mainland, he from Xian and she from Shanghai. I was introduced to them by their son, who had studied in Britain, married an English lady and settled there. Their parents were proud of him but missed him badly. They had almost no family in Taiwan; they had left most of their family behind in China. They lived in a modest house in southwest Taipei. Like most Mainlanders older than forty, they did not speak Taiwanese. Mr Chang explained his father had been a judge in X'ian and he planned to follow in his footsteps; so he chose to study law. Then came the civil war. Since Mr Chang's father worked for the Kuomintang government, he did not dare to stay; he had to flee with his family to Taiwan — a journey of 1,600 kilometers — which they made by road, rail and ship. "I lost my home, my family and my future," he said.

In climate, cuisine, history and customs, X'ian had little in common with Taiwan. I sensed that, despite having lived there for thirty years, he felt an outsider and would have preferred to return to his former life. He loved to talk about Buddhism and religion and the culture of X'ian. "It is sad materialism has replaced virtue as the main aim of people in Taiwan," he said. The culture shock was not so severe for his wife. Thousands of Shanghai people had fled to Taiwan; she seemed to have more friends and colleagues. But she talked sadly of her son, who paid one trip a year with his wife but did not intend to return to

Taiwan. She was grateful for the comfort and stability of Taipei—but this was not the life that she had prepared for. I found many children of Mainland families studied abroad, especially in the United States, and settled there. If your family belonged to the Kuomintang elite, you had the money, connections and education to do this. Perhaps they felt anxious about the future of Taiwan—would the communists take over one day? Or would the Kuomintang lose power to a party that wanted an independent state?

As time passed, I came to know my teachers better. They were Mainlanders from educated families, whose mother tongue was Mandarin. They expressed sentiments similar to those of the Changs, if not so forcefully. But they could look at the exile in another way—their life in Taiwan was immeasurably better than the one they would have had if they had stayed in China, especially those from families in the Kuomintang government and military.

One teacher, Mr Liang, liked to describe his former life as a child in Beijing—a spacious house with servants and a garden. He talked about the Imperial Palace and the narrow streets and hutongs around it, which made the city unique. His father owned large estates in Shanxi Province. I think if the Kuomintang had won the civil war, he would not have had to work but could have lived comfortably from the family wealth.

Another was a former Air Force captain who used to write and read the broadcasts from Taiwan to the Mainland. I said that, during World War II, his life must have been very dangerous, fighting superior Japanese jet fighters. "Not at all," he said. "For that very reason, our planes were grounded during the air raids. My job was flying around VIPs and playing poker."

Another teacher, Madam Yang, was also from Beijing. When no one else was in the room, she talked about the corruption in the government. "A single group controls everything and, of course, you have corruption. They have too much privilege. They would have us believe the Kuomintang and the government are the same. They are not." When a colleague came in, she changed the subject. This was a matter everyone knew about but could not discuss in public. She spoke of a Mainlander civil servant from a wealthy family who had bought land and several properties in downtown Taipei. He was challenged by a colleague who asked, "Why are you spending this money in Taiwan? We are going back to China. Does this mean you do not believe the promise of the President to return?" She said that, out of loyalty or lack of money, some Mainland families did not buy property in Taiwan and only rented. Time, of course, proved the civil servant to be correct and far-sighted. By the 1990s, his properties were worth tens of millions of New Taiwan dollars. Those who were too 'loyal' were left to regret their decision; they had no property of their own in a city that was becoming increasingly expensive.

At the end of 1981, after six months in the International Hostel, I decided to move into an apartment, for a change of scene. The rent was $54 a month. It was in Shi Da Lu (Street of Taipei Normal University). It was a crowded urban area, close to Dingzhou Street with many shops and restaurants, some open until late in the evening. There were shoe repairmen and two shops selling betel nuts. It was an easy place to live. My drink of choice of papaya milk shake; there was a stall on Dingzhou street that sold it at all hours. Our rooms were spacious. From the window of my bedroom, I could see the kitchen of the apartment in the adjoining block. A few meters away was a narrow street typical of Taipei: four- to five-story apartment blocks with small trees and plants on the balcony. On the ground floor, some rooms had been converted into restaurants or offices.

Many such streets survive today, in part because of laws that require at least 75 percent of residents to agree to a redevelopment plan. This is not good news for property developers. Today, even in expensive downtown areas, you can find down side streets wooden homes built in the Japanese period (1895-1945). Despite their age and, we imagine, lucrative offers from developers, the residents have decided to stay. In March 2023, I revisited Shi Da Lu. A short distance away was an expressway built after I had left; it involved demolition of many buildings. It was no longer a pleasant neighborhood. There was a loud noise from the cars on the expressway. The apartments in my old block all had steel bars around their front window. Dingzhou Street has added convenience stores and coffee shops — which now outnumber tea houses in Taipei.

The roommates in my apartment were an interesting group — Tomi from Okinawa, Andrew, a British student, and Sally whose family lived in a farm in Taichung in central Taiwan. She was secretary to the head of the national television company. She was adventurous and independent to choose to live with three foreign men. Her family was an example of Taiwan's progress. She had five brothers and sisters; all but one of the children graduated from university — one became a lawyer, one a teacher, one went into business and two worked in trading companies. "Sally is very relaxed among us foreign devils. As soon as she comes home, she puts on her pajamas, as is the habit here, and curls up on the sofa to look at all the funny magazines we bring back," I wrote in a letter in January 1982.

Each of us had our own room; we had a kitchen, sitting room and bathroom. The apartment was close to downtown and National Taiwan University. A short, intense man, Tomi had been in Taipei six years studying traditional Chinese medicine. I asked him what it was like to be a Japanese in Taiwan. He became angry and said, "No, I am not a Japanese. I am Okinawan." I needed to do research to understand this remark. Okinawa is 640 kilometers south of the island of Kyushu and had been a separate kingdom for most of its history. In 1879, Japan annexed the entire archipelago, abolished the monarch and forced the former king to live in Tokyo. The new rulers set about 'Japanizing' their new colony, at the expense of its language and culture. During World War II, one quarter of the civilian population — 149,000 people — died or committed suicide during devastating battles between Japanese and American forces from April to June 1945. After World War II, the Okinawans found themselves home to half the American bases in the whole of Japan, covering a large part of their territory. What had they done to deserve this?

Tomi distinguished himself one day when we found rats scurrying around the apartment. Andrew and I were paralyzed; Tomi, who was half our size, did not hesitate a moment. He filled a bucket with water and waited for the animals to appear. He picked them up with his hands and threw them into the bucket. We thanked him for dealing so efficiently with the problem. "Do not mention it," he said. "I grew up on a farm. We did this all the time."

The story of the apartment was the story of two romances. Andrew had studied Mandarin for one year in London and come to Taiwan to improve it. He had made good progress in his studies and enjoyed living in Taipei. He had a Taiwan girlfriend called Jamie; their relationship was becoming serious. Suddenly Jamie announced she had received a visa from the US to study at an American university and would leave Taiwan a month later. Of Taiwanese who went there, 85 percent did not return. This meant, in effect, the end of their relationship. Andrew was devastated. He knew of her application to study in the US, but her grandfather had refused to sponsor her, saying that, having already obtained an MA, she did not need any more education and should marry. Evidently, he had changed his mind, or Jamie had found another sponsor. Andrew was so upset that, a few months later, he decided to leave Taiwan and return to Britain. I felt sad for him. It was clear that, for Jamie, he was the number two choice. If she had not earned the US university place, she would have stayed with him. If he had been American, it might have been a different story. In the event, after six months in the US, she married another Taiwan student there.

The romance of Sally was more dramatic. She had moved from Taichung to Taipei to study at university. After graduation, she found a good job. Her sweetheart was an actor in a Beijing Opera troupe. She took Andrew and me to watch one of his performances and meet him afterwards. Lacking the proper knowledge and background of the story, we found it hard to follow. But we were impressed by the technical and artistic quality of the performance; we enjoyed meeting the young man, still in costume and his face covered in thick red, white and black makeup. The preparation must have taken hours. One Friday, Sally assembled us three roommates and said, "Tomorrow my parents are coming from Taichung for a visit. You must stay out of the apartment for the whole day, until seven in the evening." We surmised that she did not want her parents to see that she shared an apartment with three foreign men. Andrew and I spent an enjoyable Saturday in the city; it had nice department stores, restaurants, parks and museums. We returned a little after seven.

Sally was slumped on the sofa, her head in her hands. She looked devastated. That day she had taken her parents to meet her boyfriend for the first time for lunch. After he left, they had told her that she could not marry a husband from a Mainland family. If she did, she would lose contact with her family. It was an impossible choice. She said she had not finally decided what to do, but, probably, she would have to leave the young man—

her large family was too important to her. This event was, for me, the most dramatic example of the division between Taiwanese and Mainlanders, which my colleague at CEN had told me never to mention.

Later, a male friend told me his parents would, like those of Sally, oppose his marrying a girl from a Mainland family. "There is the language problem. My family speaks Taiwanese, and most of the Mainlanders do not." Even after living here thirty-two years, I asked.

"Firstly, they did not expect to stay long. Second, many are soldiers who have always lived in military compounds with their own schools, so there was no occasion to learn Taiwanese. Third, many are snobbish and look down on us and our language. They depend on the government for their livelihood, so they do not need to use Taiwanese or mix with us. This is not so true for the younger generation. For their careers, they need to mix more. Also they have grown up with us. Still, I reckon that only 60 percent of the Mainlanders have some knowledge of Taiwanese." I heard similar stories from other people, of Taiwan parents opposing marriages of their daughters with men from the Mainland. The gap in language and way of thinking was too wide. It was worse if the Mainland husband did not learn Taiwanese and mixed rarely, if at all, with his in-laws. His heart remained in his home place in the Mainland.

In the era of martial law, it was difficult to find out the reasons for the deep resentment of Sally's parents and Taiwanese like them. The subject was taboo. In the years that followed, I was gradually able to put the pieces together. Today everything is out in the open. You can buy history books that describe it. There is a 2-28 (February 28) Memorial Museum in a park opposite the Presidential Palace. In the city centre, it is a popular spot for people to walk, play music, enjoy the flowers and escape from the concrete jungle. The museum gives a detailed description of what happened, including photographs and a list of names of those killed by the security forces.

At the end of World War II, the six million Taiwanese welcomed the Chinese troops. The formal surrender of the Japanese army on the island took place in a large auditorium in downtown Taipei on October 25, 1945. While they had been a colony of Japan for fifty years, the Taiwanese were happy to be reunited with their mother country. The government in Nanjing sent civil and military officials to run the island, led by Chen Yi, Garrison Commander and Chief Executive. Differences between them and local people quickly surfaced. Only a minority of Taiwan people spoke Mandarin, the new official language, but their languages were Taiwanese, Hakka and Japanese. Chen spoke fluent Japanese but refused to use it in talking to Taiwan people.

The new administration adopted piecemeal Japan's colonial system and took over the companies it had established. They controlled the island's main products, including sugar, tobacco, camphor and alcohol. The administration brought in Mainlanders to run the government and manage these companies. Taiwan people, especially the elite, strongly objected. Many were more educated than the newcomers and knew the products better. Of the three hundred sixteen staff in Chen Yi's office, just seventeen were Taiwanese; of seventeen city and county mayors, three were Taiwanese. In 1946, Chen Yi banned Japanese newspapers and magazines—rendering the population illiterate; 75 percent of Taiwanese could speak and read Japanese. There was a shortage of teachers of Mandarin. The new rulers exported Taiwan rice and other food to Shanghai and other Mainland cities for a healthy profit. Inflation in Taiwan soared, as did unemployment. Taiwan people demanded the democracy promised in China's constitution. But the government held no election there in 1947, as it did in the rest of China.

The spark that set off the tinderbox was struck on the evening of February 27, 1947. In downtown Taipei, a six-member team from the Taiwan Tobacco Monopoly (TTM) confiscated the smuggled cigarettes of a forty-year-old lady hawker (Lin Jiang-mai, 林江邁) and struck her, drawing blood. A large crowd attacked the team, who fled for their lives. One of them opened fire, injuring a man who died the next day. On February 28, the crowd sacked the TTM office and wounded three of the staff; one later died. The crowd demonstrated in front of the office of Chen Yi. Military police opened fire, causing casualties. This set off a rebellion—shops and factories closed and students boycotted classes. Young activists broadcast news of the clashes on the radio and the revolt spread all over the island. There were armed confrontations between Taiwanese and the security forces. Chen Yi requested additional troops to put down the rebellion; President Chiang Kai-shek agreed, and they arrived on March 8. During the crackdown that followed, the security forces killed 10,000 to 20,000 Taiwanese. They especially targeted the elite who were well educated, had administrative experience and professional skills; they could have formed an alternative ruling class. Many fled to Japan and the United States, which became the center of those campaigning for Taiwan independence.

Angry at how Chen Yi had mismanaged Taiwan, Chiang dismissed him in April 1947 and sent him to a post in the Mainland. In April 1950, he arrested Chen on charges of collaborating with the victorious communist armies. In May 1950, a military court in Taipei sentenced him to death; he was executed on June 18. On May 20, 1949, President Chiang declared martial law in Taiwan. It was still in force when I arrived. The quelling of the rebellion started what Taiwan people call the 'White Terror'—officers of the TGC (Taiwan Garrison Command, the secret police) detained people they suspected of supporting independence or working for the communists. Taiwan people told me the TGC agents often came, in plainclothes, to make arrests in the middle of the night. Suspects were sentenced in military courts. They were held in camps and prisons. Sometimes, the TGC flew them over the Pacific and tossed them out of the planes. Scholars estimate that, during the White Terror, about 2,000 people were executed and 8,000 were sentenced to long prison terms.

These tragic events created a deep division between the native Taiwanese who accounted for about 80 percent percent of the population and the twenty 2 percent of Mainlanders who ruled them. No wonder it could not be spoken of. Like Ivan, Henry and Emily, Sally had received her education in the 1960s and 1970s. They all spoke Mandarin fluently and had Mainlander classmates. So, for them, the division was less bitter. But Sally's parents had personal experience of the 1947 uprising and its suppression; they could not forget and forgive. Sally told her parents her boyfriend had played no part in the terrible events of the late 1940s and 1950s; like her, he was a student who became an adult in the late 1970s. But their hatred of the Mainlanders was too deep to accept him as their son-in-law.

One social highlight of 1982 was the evening of St Patrick's Day in a Taipei bar. This is what I wrote a few days later in a letter to a family member: "I gathered with five Irish Columban missionaries and a large number of other RC priests, young and old, for a celebration. What good craic (repartee) it was, as they say in Belfast. Many had talents as singer, dancers and tellers of lewd stories. The older ones worked first on the Mainland, before the communists threw them out in 1949/1950. Many were subjected to a public trial, at which those closest to them were called to testify against them. It was a bitter and humiliating experience.

"These priests are unlike other foreigners here. This is where they will live for the rest of their lives; their commitment is total. The rest of us seem like robbers and opportunists only. They are regarded with some suspicion by this very strict government. Some of the priests concern themselves with labor and political rights; if they do, they are not allowed to come back if they leave. But the authorities stop short of throwing them out, as it does not want to create an international incident. It is within that margin that they have to operate."

One of the Irish Columbans who had excellent in Mandarin was Father Edward Kelly, who had been a missionary in Hsinchu since 1978. He became a supporter of democracy in Taiwan and started to collect journals and magazines published by the opposition. In 1983, he moved from Taiwan to Hong Kong. The talk was that the government did not approve of his political work but did not want to expel him. So his leaving for Hong Kong was a compromise solution.

3

THE LOVE AFFAIR WITH JAPAN

In a Taipei pharmacy, I was waiting for the salesman to give plasters for a cut. While his hands searched for the plasters, his eyes were glued to something on his right.

"Good to watch?" I asked.

"Oh yes, this is the final day of the autumn Basho Sumo Tournament in Tokyo. I cannot miss a bout," he said.

I peered around the counter and saw a television showing live coverage of the tournament, with commentary in Japanese; it was not visible from the street. Funny, I thought, the four channels in Taiwan were Mandarin only. He saw what I was thinking and said with a smile, "This is what we call the fifth channel, NHK via satellite. Many people watch it. We are not supposed to, but the government turns a blind eye." That was my first awakening of what many called 'Taiwan's love affair with Japan'.

Many native Taiwanese had a positive view of Japanese colonial rule, even more so after the behavior of the Nationalist government in its first fifteen years after arrival. Japanese had been the language of government, education and business for fifty years. Many people spoke it; they had developed a taste for Japanese films, books, magazines and culture—including Sumo. After the end of World War II, more than 90 percent cent of the 300,000 Japanese residents of Taiwan were repatriated.

But personal ties continued between some of them and their friends and former students in Taiwan. Teachers came back for emotional reunions. Classmates gathered to write haiku poems. I found shops in Taipei selling exclusively Japanese books, while convenience shops offered Japanese magazines on fashion, travel, culture and cuisine. While the United States was the primary destination for students going abroad after 1945, Japan was a strong second.

In 1985, a Buddhist charity, the Tzu Chi Foundation, was raising funds to build a hospital in Hualien, east Taiwan, the poorest part of the island. A wealthy Japanese real estate developer arrived and offered the charity the extraordinary sum of $200 million, to cover the entire construction cost. A devout Buddhist, he had grown up in Hualien and had a great fondness for the town. He wanted to show his gratitude to Taiwan for allowing its Japanese residents return safely to Japan at the end of World War II and not seek wartime reparations, a decision that had greatly helped its swift reconstruction.

At a dinner in Taipei in March 2023, two guests neatly summarized this 'love affair' with Japan. David Tanaka, a professor of Japanese, said the contrast between Korea and Taiwan was astonishing. "In Korea, students are taught to hate Japan and see nothing positive during its forty-year rule. Here it is the opposite. But they were the same Japanese." Two places away at the same table, Eric Chou, a businessman from a Mainland family, said, "Many Taiwan people think they are second-generation Japanese."

The Japanese imprint is there for all to see, starting with the imposing Presidential Palace in central Taipei that was the office of the Governor-General until August 1945. There was a similar imposing building in central Seoul for its Governor General, but, in 1995 and 1996, the South Korean government demolished it as a symbol of colonial rule. Other important government structures in use today in Taipei were built by the Japanese, including the office of the Prime Minister, the Control Yuan, the National Taiwan Museum, the National Taiwan University Hospital and the Taipei Guest House, where the government receives foreign leaders.

Japanese rule of Taiwan did not start smoothly. Many Taiwan people did not accept the decision of a dynasty in distant Beijing to hand them over to the Japanese Empire without their consent, after its disastrous defeat in the 1894-95 war. Just over a month after Beijing signed the treaty giving up the island, its residents proclaimed the 'Taiwan Democratic State' (臺灣民主國). The declaration of independence read: "The Japanese have affronted China by annexing our territory of Formosa, as the supplications of us, the people of Formosa, to the portals of the Throne have been made in vain. We now learn that the Japanese slaves are about to arrive." It acknowledged the suzerainty of China over Taiwan. But they were no match for Asia's most modern army that arrived soon after and put down the rebellion. Unlike the Qing Dynasty in a feudal country that had long resisted demands for reform, Japan was a modern state. It brought to its new colony the benefits of modernization—an extensive network of running water for Taipei, a financial system, construction of ports and railways, six sugar refineries, hydro-electric power stations, modern hospitals and compulsory education. By 1904, Taiwan had become economically self-sufficient and required no more subsidies from Tokyo. By 1943, 71.3 percent of school-age children were receiving education. If Taiwan had not been ruled by Japan, it would have been part of China. The first four decades of 20th Century China were a period of revolution, battles between rival warlords, a civil war, and then invasion by Japan. As a colony, Taiwan enjoyed relative peace and development unknown in most of China. Scholars estimate that by 1940, Taiwan society was thirty years in advance of that in most of China.

The Calvary for Taiwan came during the last eight years of Japanese rule, after its all-out invasion of China in July 1937. In Taiwan as in Korea, the government launched a movement known as 皇民化 (huangminhua) that aimed to turn the citizens into Japanese. They could speak only Japanese at school and had to worship the Emperor and attend Shinto shrines. They were encouraged to adopt Japanese names and wear Japanese clothes. More than 80,000 joined the military; more than 30,000 were killed, including Lee Teng-chin, elder brother of Lee Teng-hui. Teng-chin died on February 15, 1945, when US planes bombed his vessel in Manila Harbor. In November 1943, the American Air Force began to bomb Taiwan; it spread all over the island in the twelve months leading to Japan's surrender on August 15, 1945. On November 27, 1943, the leaders of China, Britain and the United States met in Cairo and decided that, after the end of the war, Taiwan would be returned to China; its people were not consulted.

Taiwan people are not alone in having positive feelings for the former colonial power. Many Africans cherish the language, culture and education of Britain and France, especially when their governments have not delivered the improvements promised at the time of independence. If the KMT takeover of Taiwan had been less violent, this affection for Japan would surely have diminished. Many Taiwanese saw one colonial master replaced by another—"the dogs left, but the pigs came" was a common saying. But the KMT government did far better than most African regimes, delivering economic growth and better standards of living. As it did, so this resentment declined. Today marriages between children of Mainland and local families are commonplace, and not a matter for comment.

When I lived in Taipei, I often went with friends to Peitou, a lovely hot spring resort on the side of a mountain north of the city that had been developed by the Japanese. What I saw were traditional wooden houses and lovely baths, like those of Hakone and Ibusuki in Japan. One day we walked along Wenchuan Road (温泉路) and my friends pointed out this was the Chinese word for 'hot spring'. What none of us could have imagined was that a large building back from the road, Number 144, was the headquarters of a team of Japanese military advisers — not during World War II, but after it!

Known as the White Group, it was established by President Chiang Kai-shek in 1949 and not disbanded until 1969. It took its name from the Chinese nom de guerre of its leader Pai Hong-liang (白鴻亮); 'bai' in Chinese means white. His real name was Tomita Naosuke, a major-general in the Imperial Japanese Army (IJA). Between December 1944 and August 1945, he was Deputy Chief of Staff and then Chief of Staff of the 23rd Army in China. In 1949, he and sixteen other former Japanese officers were smuggled into Taiwan via Hong Kong or flown from the Mainland. Over the next twenty years, they trained at least 10,000 Kuomintang soldiers in Taiwan. After the group was disbanded, Tomita continued to live in the house on Wenchuan Road. He was made an honorary general of the Republic of China, the only foreigner to receive this honor. He died in 1979 on a visit to Tokyo; his ashes were divided between Japan and Taiwan. In 2014, a Japanese tour group, including relatives of officers in the White Group, visited the house to express their respects to Tomita on the 35th anniversary of his death. When I asked members of Kuomintang families why they had lost the civil war, they had the same answer — the Japanese invasion. So how could their leader invite an enemy general to train his soldiers?

The answer lies in the personal life of President Chiang. In

1907, at the age of twenty, he went to study in a preparatory school for the IJA in Tokyo and then served two years in that army from 1909 to 1911. He greatly admired the discipline, physical training and obedience of the Japanese soldier, as well as their customs of bathing in cold water and eating cold food. He saw clearly why the Japanese military had become the most powerful in Asia, defeating first China and then Tsarist Russia — the first victory by an Asian army over a major European power. For the rest of his life, Chiang followed habits acquired in Japan — a strict routine, rising at 5:00 a.m., eating simple meals and going to bed early.

In September 1949, while Chiang was still fighting in the Mainland, he signed a secret agreement with members of the White Group to advise him on strategy against the victorious communists. They were given a lucrative salary and bonuses for their families. In November 1949, some were flown from Sichuan to Taiwan and, less than two weeks later, Chiang followed them.

What Chiang wanted in Taiwan from these Japanese veterans was training to improve the quality of his soldiers. They also introduced reserve officer exams and close combat techniques. The existence of the group had to be kept secret, since the US opposed it. Also it ran counter to the 'de-Japanization' of the population that was the official policy; most of the 1.5 million who had come with Chiang from the Mainland despised the Japanese for atrocities they had committed in China during the war. In 2023, I asked a Japanese deputy manager at a hotel in Taipei how people in Taiwan had treated her. "When I was studying here, most people were polite. Then I met an elderly man who had served in the military. He shouted at me and said, 'You Japanese killed so many people in China. You have no right to be here. Go back to Japan.' Not everyone is so favorable to Japanese."

Japanese imprints are all over Taiwan. One is baseball, the

most popular spectator sport in the island. The colonists brought it to the island and it became very popular. In 1931, the Chiayi School of Agriculture and Forestry, from southwest Taiwan, took second place in the Pan-Japanese High School Baseball Tournament. This passion continued after the Japanese departed. Between 1969 and 1982, Taiwan won thirteen Little League World Series championships. In their honor, the Central Bank in 2000 issued a new NT$500 note showing the young baseball players celebrating their victory. Top Taiwan baseball stars go on to the major leagues in Japan and the United States. The most famous is Wang Chen-chi, or Sadaharu Oh in Japanese. He holds the world record for the most home runs ever hit by a professional player — 868. He was the third bat of the Yomiuri Giants of Tokyo when they won the Japanese championship for nine consecutive years from 1965 to 1973; he also won championships as a manager. Wang was born in May 1940 in Tokyo, where his father managed a noodle shop. Throughout his life, he has carried a RoC passport and supported baseball in Taiwan. In 2001, the Taiwan government appointed him as ambassador without portfolio to promote sport and exchanges between the two sides.

In September 1972, Tokyo recognized the People's Republic and cut relations with Taipei. It was a severe diplomatic blow — nearly seven years before the United States did the same thing — but non-official relations continued to flourish. When I lived there, the embassy had been replaced by the Interchange Association; it operated out of the premises of the former embassy and included a Japanese Cultural Center. It functioned as a de facto embassy; a similar office in the second city, Kaohsiung, acted as a de facto consulate. The arrangement worked well and has continued until today. It became known as the 'Japanese formula' and was used by other countries that later recognized Beijing and broke diplomatic relations with Taipei — but retained ties in all other fields.

Before September 1972, the RoC had an embassy in Tokyo, in the Minato District, one of the most expensive in the city. After the break in relations, the site was handed over to the People's Republic. But, I learned later, this did not need to happen. In the 1990s, when I was posted in Tokyo, I came to know staff of the Association of East Asian Relations (AEAR); this was the de facto embassy of Taiwan in Japan and the counterpart of the Interchange Association.

One explained to me that, in the early 1970s, their diplomats in Tokyo realized what was going to happen and that the Japanese government would switch from Taipei to Beijing. So they informed President Chiang Kai-shek and urged him to sell the embassy land and building to a private entity. This would mean that, when the switch occurred, the Japanese government could not give the site to Beijing since it belonged to a private owner. It would have to find another site for Beijing to build its new embassy. "But the President was very stubborn. He said that, after all he had done for Japan, it would never make such a switch." He would not consider such a sale. So, when the switch came, Taiwan lost its extremely valuable real estate; it was handed over to Beijing, which built a new embassy on the site. It was Taipei that had to find another site and build a new office there. Land in central Tokyo was always expensive.

"But we learned our lesson," the official said. "When the same thing happened in the United States in 1978, we saved our building." The new President, Chiang Ching-kuo, was more in touch with the world. It was in 1947 that the RoC purchased an estate named Twin Oaks, a twenty-six-room English Georgian Renaissance-style mansion on 7.38 hectares in northwest Washington, built in 1888. It became its embassy in the US. In late 1978, with the switch of Washington to Beijing imminent, the Taiwan government sold the site to the Friends of Free China Association, an American non-profit. So the US government had to provide the PRC with a new site for its embassy in Washington. In 1979, the US Congress passed the Taiwan Relations Act, which provided legal protection for the original ownership. So, in 1982, the Taiwan government bought back Twin Oaks. So, with a four-year break from 1978 to 1982, it has served as Taiwan's main office in the United States since World War II. It is an ideal site for receptions on the National Days of the two countries and to host visiting VIPs

Later in Tokyo, I had the opportunity to interview the head of the AEAR. It was Alex Chiang Hsiao-wu, second son of Chiang Ching-kuo and Faina, his Russian wife. He was an unusual choice for one of the most important positions in Taiwan's Foreign Service. He did not speak Japanese and had served only four years as a diplomat in Singapore from 1986-1990. The diplomatic gossip was that he had been sent to Tokyo by then President Lee Teng-hui to get him out of Taiwan and prevent him from organizing opposition to Lee. His office was in a modern office building in the south of Tokyo.

In the interview, Chiang explained that his was a difficult job, because Japanese officials above the level of deputy section chief were not allowed to see him or his staff. "We face many obstacles and difficulties. But, due to the hard work of the staff here, we have friends in many circles in Japan, especially in the Parliament," he said. Of the seven hundred sixty members of Japan's Parliament, two hundred twenty belonged to the pro-Taiwan Japan-China Association. The interview revealed no news about bilateral relations nor the Chiang family, but the photographer was delighted. Chiang's office was full of photographs of his famous father and grandfather, so the photographer was able to take elegant shots with all three members of the dynasty in the same frame. Chiang held the office for just over a year before being replaced by someone better qualified, Hsu Shui-teh. A native Taiwanese, he spoke fluent Japanese after six years at primary school in the colonial era and eighteen months at a university in Tokyo. He served as Mayor of Taipei and Kaohsiung. In the absence of official relations, the Taiwan representative and his staff must work through private channels, using associations of friendly legislators, academics and others. If he meets Japanese officials, he must be discreet and avoid the notice of Chinese officials looking for any hint of recognition.

My friends and I often went to Peitou, the hot spring resort. Close to the town center was an elegant two-story wooden building of Japanese design that now houses the Peitou Museum. As we looked at the exhibits, I noticed a photograph of Hirohito, then Crown Prince of Japan, visiting Taiwan in April 1923. In November 1921, he had become Crown Prince because of the mental incapacity of his father, the Taisho Emperor. In 1922, he toured Britain and five other European countries, becoming the first Japanese Crown Prince to go abroad. This visit to Taiwan was similarly the first visit by a Crown Prince to a colony. Staring at his expressionless face, I was astonished. Such a photograph is unimaginable in any other country in Asia occupied by the Japanese military; this was the Emperor who oversaw the invasion of China, the Nanjing Massacre and many other atrocities. My friends told me the museum had been built in 1921 as the Kazan Hotel, a club for officers of the Imperial Japanese Army. During World War II, kamikaze pilots stayed there during their last night on earth.

Walking through Peitou, it did not take long to see the deep Japanese imprint. Prior to the Japanese arrival in 1895, the Aboriginal inhabitants had enjoyed sulfur baths; a German merchant opened the first hot spring club. The Japanese took it to another level. They built inns and hot mineral baths and a railway line to bring residents from Taipei; it ran from 1916 until 1988, before being replaced by a new subway station that opened in March 1997. Some of the inns were reserved for Japanese military and civilian officials; others were open to the general public. One villa had an air-raid shelter built of reinforced concrete during World War II, in case of an American air raid. The Japanese brought the entertainment provided at home — drinking, geishas, musical performances and lady companions. During the war years from 1940 to 1945, Japanese soldiers and civilians came to Peitou for 'rest and recreation'. Taiwan people eagerly embraced the custom of hot spring baths. The town offered a variety of choice, from public baths to hotels medium-range and expensive; some offered baths in the rooms.

For an inquisitive person like myself, public baths are an excellent venue for chatting. One proverb in Japanese says "in nudity, there is truth." This means that naked in the hot tub together, the chairman of Toyota and the street cleaner are equal. They are also relaxed, away from their normal stress of office or home; since your companion will not see you again, he can be more open. So, in the pools of Peitou, I used to ask the other bathers about their lives and opinions. The most memorable came in an establishment called Tokyo, built during the colonial period and exactly like those in a Japanese city. My neighbor was an elderly man; from his accent, I could tell was a native Taiwanese, not a Mainlander.

"Do you know, when my sister was looking for a husband, what was the most important qualification?" he asked. "In those days, marriages were arranged by families, so the parents of both sides had to approve. Fluency in Japanese was the number one factor. With that, she could find a good husband... I wish Taiwan was still part of Japan. Then the US Sixth Fleet would be patrolling the Taiwan Strait and we would not have to listen to China constantly threatening to take us over. This makes us very angry. China has nothing to do with us."

In Japan, as in other countries, the entertainment industry, including hot spring baths, is connected to sex. A weekend in a nice hotel in Peitou is an excellent gift to a partner. The warm, relaxed ambience makes everyone more relaxed and amorous. In 1956, the government legalized prostitution in Peitou, on condition the guest in a hotel requested a lady. They were delivered by a man on a scooter, winding up the narrow roads on the mountain. During the Vietnam War, American soldiers were stationed in Taiwan, and thousands more came from the front for rest and recreation. Prostitution in Peitou became big business.

News of it even reached a British university friend of mine. During a visit to Taipei, he insisted a night in Peitou be included in his itinerary. As his host, I accompanied him in the taxi to a large hotel, with dozens of rooms. He told the man at the reception desk what he wanted and went to his room. Fifteen minutes later, a man on the scooter arrived with his passenger; she was given the room number and took the lift. While I read a magazine and sipped tea in the large front hall, more ladies arrived. Yes, this was the 'oldest profession in the world', but it was depressing all the same. Men from the US, Britain and Japan came all this way to meet young ladies with whom they could not communicate. After an hour, my friend's lady appeared again and left on the scooter. My friend arrived, chipper despite the late hour. He traveled a lot for his work—I think he was collecting 'scores' from different continents.

In December 1967, American TIME magazine published a photograph of a 21-year-old G.I. in a hot bath in a Peitou hotel being looked after by two young ladies; all were naked. The article below it said the town had seventy-five hotels, with thousands of G.I.s visiting every year. The Taiwan government was very embarrassed at this image of their land as a sex destination for foreigners. The Vietnam War ended in April 1975 and the US broke diplomatic relations with the RoC on January 1, 1979, so there were no longer American soldiers based on the island. The Taiwan government outlawed prostitution in 1979. In 1984, I interviewed an officer in a department responsible for attracting Taiwan's students abroad, mainly in the US, to come home to work; it was part of a national effort to upgrade Taiwan's manufacturing through the skills and experience these students had gained overseas. "Of course, we did not want to encourage prostitution," he said. "But we were like other poor countries. We had to earn foreign exchange where we could. Now the economy is stronger, our exports are higher and we no longer need to exploit our women in this way." Friends in Taipei told me that, of course, prostitution had not disappeared. It had moved to hotels and guest houses in the city — but more discreet and never on the mass scale of the 1960s. As in other countries, it remained part of 'business travel' — clients who flew in from abroad were given a lavish dinner, drinks and then offered ladies. It cost about $20 to pay a lady to sit with you, pour drinks and dance. Taiwan residents needing services did not need to look hard — nightclubs or massage parlors and barber shops with whirling multi-coloured signs outside.

One day, at Taipei International Airport, I was flipping through titles in a bookstore. One was about individuals who had made major historical contributions to Taiwan. To my surprise, I found two Japanese names — Shinpei Goto and Yoichi Hatta. Goto was the first civilian governor of Taiwan, serving from 1898 to 1906. A medical doctor, Goto revolutionized the island's medical system. When he arrived, bubonic plague, cholera and malaria were widespread. He set up quarantine stations at the ports and ordered the public to report cases to the authorities; he enacted a quarantine program. He started a campaign to catch rats that carried the plague; between 1904 and 1908, as many as 4.6 million were caught each year. By 1917, bubonic plague had been eliminated from Taiwan.

Goto also built a new water and sewage system for Taipei. To deal with widespread opium addiction, he ordered that it could only be purchased from licensed retailers. Thanks to strict enforcement, the number of addicts fell from 165,000 in 1900 to fewer than 8,000 by 1941. Goto also developed the production of sugar, salt, tobacco and camphor and invested in roads, ports, railways and post offices. By 1904, Taiwan was economically self-supporting and no longer required a subsidy from Japan. The National Taiwan Museum in Taipei has a full-size bronze statue of Goto.

The achievements of Yoichi Hatta are no less remarkable. He moved to Taiwan in 1910 after his graduation from university and remained there for his entire life. Between 1920 and 1930, he oversaw construction of the Wushantou Reservoir and Chianan Irrigation Waterway Chiayi and Tainan counties in southwest Taiwan. Completed in 1930, the reservoir was the largest in Asia at the time. The irrigation system covered 10,000 square kilometers of waterway and watered 150,000 hectares of farmland. It transformed the livelihood of the farmers and greatly increased their output. "It remains a masterpiece of irrigation construction," says the Ministry of Culture on its website. "Its three-rotation system allowed three times more farmers to utilize the irrigation system." In 2011, a memorial park in Hatta's honor opened near the reservoir, with a statue of him. The statue was created in 1931, showing him in work clothes deep in thought. After the war, the Chianan Irrigation Association hid it because of anti-Japanese sentiment in the ruling Nationalist Party. They were finally able to put it back in 1981. Then, in the spring of 2017, anti-Japanese activists removed its head; the Tainan government ordered a new one, which visitors can see in the memorial park. President Ma Ying-jeou, of the Kuomintang, and Tsai Ing-wen, of the rival Democratic Progressive Party, have both gone to the statue to pay their respects.

One reason Japan took over Taiwan, like Manchuria thirty-six years later, was to move surplus population overseas. It set up Immigrant Villages in Taiwan; the first one was in 1899 for one hundred thirty-three families in the eastern county of Hualien. During the colonial period, thousands of Japanese farmers moved to Taiwan, primarily growing rice, sugar and tobacco. After the surrender, all were repatriated to Japan, but visitors can still see the remains of three of the villages — Yoshino, Toyota and Hayashida, all in Hualien County. The remains include crumbling Japanese-style houses, a Buddhist Yoshino Shrine and a stele that commemorates the founding of Yoshino. Just as with the photograph of Crown Prince Hirohito in the Peitou Museum, it is unimaginable that any other government of a country occupied by the Japanese military would allow such relics to remain.

The most dramatic example of the feeling of Taiwan people for Japan came after the terrible earthquake and tsunami that hit northeast Japan on March 11, 2011. With a population of twenty-three million, Taiwan donated more money than any other land, including the combined amount given by United States and South Korea, with populations of 331 million and 49 million, respectively.

Taiwan donated more than $170 million, or $7 per individual Taiwanese, with 90 percent coming from individual donors. The Yomiuri Shimbun, Japan's largest-selling newspaper, carried a full-page advertisement, paid for by a Japanese travel agency, to express appreciation for the generosity of Taiwanese people. The government of Taiwan sent a rescue team and relief goods. President Ma Ying-jeou personally donated $7,000 and took part in a telethon to urge people to donate as much as they could; he operated one of the call-in lines. The most powerful earthquake ever recorded in Japan and the tsunami that followed killed 19,759 people, injured 6,200 and left 2,500 missing.

Another element unique to Taiwan is nostalgic films about the Japanese period. I remember a comedy about a giant whale that arrived on the beach of a village. The plot revolved around what to do with this unexpected guest. One of the main characters was a portly Japanese police sergeant who could not decide what to do. He was the opposite of the immaculately dressed and ruthless Japanese military officers I have seen in many Mainland films. The clumsiness and indecision of the sergeant was one of the main themes in the film — and very comic.

The most famous and most successful film in this genre was *Cape No 7*, by Taiwan director Wei Te-sheng, about a Japanese teacher who fell in love with a Taiwan woman during the colonial period. After the surrender in 1945, he was repatriated to Japan. His sweetheart planned to elope with him, but never did. He wrote her seven love letters, but could not bring himself to send them. After he passed away sixty years later, his daughter found the letters and sent them to Taiwan to the woman's old address, Cape No 7. She found and read the letters. The film proved wildly successful, becoming the second highest-grossing film in Taiwan's history after *Titanic*. While this was due in part to the excellent plot and acting, another element was the sympathy felt by many in the audience for the protagonists, whom they saw as innocent victims of the war.

Another popular film about the Japanese period was *Kano*,

released in 2014. This was based on the true story — which we described earlier in this chapter — of the Taiwan high school baseball team, which won second place in the Japanese High School Baseball Championship in 1931. The team was unique at that time because it contained Han Taiwanese, Aboriginal Taiwanese and Japanese students.

The most 'Japanese' person in Taiwan was Lee Teng-hui, who served as President from January 1988 to May 2000. In Taiwan, he remains a controversial figure, evoking admiration and hatred in equal measure. Books written about him reflect both opinions; we will describe these later in the book. Here let us describe his 'Japanese' identity. He was born in January 1923 into a farming family in Sanzhi, northwest Taiwan. His father was a police officer. His elder brother Lee Teng-chin joined the police academy and volunteered for the Imperial Japanese Navy. In July 1941, he was sent to the Philippines. He was killed in the Battle of Manila on February 15, 1945, when his warship sank after being hit by a missile from an American jet fighter. After World War II, the Japanese government registered him among its war dead in the Yasukuni Shrine in Tokyo, under the Japanese name he used. More than 30,000 Taiwanese were killed in the war serving in the Japanese military; 26,000 of them are enshrined in Yasukuni. This shrine is controversial in China and the two Koreas, the countries that suffered most under Japanese rule. They say that among those honored in the shrine are war criminals.

An outstanding student, Lee Teng-hui was one of only four Taiwan students among a class of Japanese at a top Taipei high school. In September 1943, he graduated with honors and won a scholarship to Kyoto Imperial University, to study agricultural economics. In 1944, like his fellow students, he was conscripted into the army. He had the good fortune not to be sent to the front; when the war ended, he was serving as a second lieutenant in mainland Japan.

Japanese journalists I knew interviewed Lee when he was President. They told me his Japanese was fluent and without accent; after the interview, he invited them to lunch and discuss current affairs in Japan. He knew the names of the competitors in sumo tournaments and the latest gossip in Tokyo. To acquire such knowledge, he must have watched NHK regularly — like the man in the pharmacy at the start of this chapter. The journalists were charmed by his perfect Japanese, his friendliness and knowledge of what was going on in their country — it was like talking to a Japanese, they said. Lee often used to say, "Until I was twenty-two, I was Japanese." In a legal sense, this was correct — but not an appropriate thing for the President of the Republic of China to say. It angered many people.

While Taiwanese was his mother language, Japanese was the language of his education, university and military service. It was only after the end of the war that he properly learned Mandarin and then learned English, to study at Cornell University in the United States. He had many friends among the Japanese elite, including politicians, business people and intellectuals. Prime Minister Shintaro Abe was a friend. No other Asian leader was so publicly proud of his links with Japan. A retired official who used to work under him told me Lee read books in Japanese and English, but not in Chinese. This was the President of the Republic of China! He said it was hard to translate Lee's speeches into foreign languages, because they jumped from one topic to another.

After his retirement as President in 2000, Lee continued to visit Japan regularly, despite the strong opposition of the Chinese Embassy that asked the Tokyo government not to issue a visa. Between 2000 and 2018, he went nine times. In 2001, it took a petition by more than 15,000 people, including eighty-eight professors of Kyoto University and more than 1,100 doctors, to persuade the government to give him a visa to visit his alma mater and have an operation for a heart condition by an eminent Japanese surgeon. In October that year, his supporters set up the Japan Lee Teng-hui Friendship Association to lobby with the government to allow him entry and arrange his visits. He gave speeches at universities and to members of Parliament at the Diet in Tokyo; he visited the Yasukuni Shrine to mourn his elder brother. He went to the ancestral home of Inazo Nitobe, known as 'he father of Taiwan's sugar industry' and followed the footsteps of Basho Matsue, Japan's most famous poet of haiku, who lived in the 17th Century. In his speeches, he praised Shinpei Goto, Yoichi Hatta and other Japanese who had contributed to the development of Taiwan; the speeches attracted large audiences of people delighted to hear a former foreign president speak so positively of their country. From Chinese and Korean leaders, they heard nothing but anger and criticism of the pre-1945 period. The media gave his speeches and articles wide coverage.

In 2023, I showed one to a Japanese friend in Hong Kong. She marveled, "He uses an elegant Japanese of the 1930s with words that people of my generation do not know how to use. This is a high standard." His final visit to Japan was in June 2018, to Okinawa, to remember the Taiwan soldiers buried there. He was ninety-five. After his death on July 30, 2020, former Prime Minister Yoshiro Mori led a cross-party Japanese delegation to Taipei to pay tribute to Lee; he expressed gratitude for his contributions to Japan-Taiwan relations and his support for Japan's post-war recovery.

In December 2022, Japanese scholars and representatives of Parliament attended the Taiwan-Japan Eternal Relations Forum with Taiwan counterparts in Taipei, to mark the 50th anniversary since diplomatic relations were cut. Speakers described how bilateral ties had flourished despite the lack of official relations. At the forum, Hiroyasu Izumi, head of the Japan-Taiwan Exchange Association — the de facto embassy — praised Lee Teng-hui "for strengthening Taiwan's sense of identity and building a democratic state". He also praised former Japanese Prime Minister Shintaro Abe for developing Japan-Taiwan relations. "It is sad that both men have passed away, a loss to the momentum between the two sides. But nothing can stop the forward pace. We should hold hands for the next 100 years together," he said. The most senior Japanese attending was Koichi Hagiuda, policy chief of the ruling Liberal Democratic Party. He gave the keynote speech at the forum and also went to pay his respects at the grave of Lee Teng-hui.

One day I and a friend drove to the ancestral home of Lee Teng-hui, in a rural area north of Taipei. It was a one-storey red brick home with trees in the forecourt; it was surrounded by rice paddies. I was surprised. There was nothing to indicate that this had been the family home of the former president — no photographs, no display board and no gift shop. I expressed this surprise to another visitor who had just arrived and got out of his car. He laughed loudly. "You have been in the Mainland too long," he said. "Lee was a normal person, with faults like the rest of us."

4

GOVERNANCE — '10,000-YEAR DEPUTIES' AND DISSIDENTS

I met an American journalist called Bob King who had been in Taiwan for six years. He earned a good living by writing basically the same story for the Asian Wall Street Journal, the Financial Times and an American news syndicate. He also wrote advertising copy for computer firms and government departments. He lived in a large, comfortable apartment in downtown Taipei.

"The great thing about working here is that there are no deadlines, as there are no breaking news stories," he said. "No one outside knows what is going on. So I file more or less when I please."

He composed his stories on a counterfeit computer from one of the firms he wrote for; they gave it to him for half the retail price, which was itself thirty percent of the price of the real brand. For the first five years, he paid no income tax because he was paid per article. Unfortunately for him, the tax department changed the rules and he had to pay. He spoke reasonable Mandarin but did not read the Chinese media –his girlfriend did that for him.

Bob's situation reflected Taiwan's place in the world. The hot stories in East Asia in the early 1980s were the opening of Mainland China and the rise of Japan — would Japan overtake the US and become the world's number one economic power?

Foreign journalists were concentrated in Tokyo, Beijing and Hong Kong. There were few in Taiwan outside the four global news agencies — Reuters, Agence France Presse, The Associated Press and United Press International. This opened a little window for me, despite my limited knowledge of Taiwan. Foreign news organizations with no presence there were happy to accept stories on a freelance basis. So I was able to write for newspapers in Hong Kong and the Foreign News Service of the Observer in Britain and later TIME magazine, newspapers in Japan, the BBC and UPI. I never had a scoop — the government controlled information too well for that. But working at CEN provided a good understanding of the economy. I supplemented that with what I read in other media and learned from people I talked to.

When I arrived in Taiwan, it had been a single-party state under martial law for thirty-two years. But Chiang Ching-kuo who became president in 1978, did allow limited space for the opposition. They could run as independents in elections. In local elections in November 1981, several won a large number of votes and were elected but they had no executive power. To my surprise, we could interview and write about political dissidents; they had their mail opened, telephones tapped and were followed. The government permitted this, provided journalists balanced the stories with the official point of view and also wrote about economics, culture and other topics. The police knew exactly what each journalist wrote. The important thing was to keep a balance between pro- and anti-government voices. One foreign journalist wrote only about dissidents; he was warned not to do this, but paid no heed. So, on his next visit to Hong Kong, he was not given a visa to return.

Once a friend in the government told me he had seen my dossier in the offices of the police. It was not thick, since my time in Taiwan had not been very long.

"The dossiers on the foreign journalists have details of their personal and professional lives," he said. "At the bottom is a box that the officer responsible has to tick. One box says 'pro-China' (親華) and the other 'anti-China' (反華)."

"Which one is mine?" I asked.

"You are pro-China," he said.

In the summer of 1981, Taiwan was in its thirty-second year of martial law. It was the longest such period of any country in history—Syria would surpass it in the 21st Century. But it did not feel like military rule in an African dictatorship with gun-toting soldiers patrolling the streets in front of terrified people. While there were police stations all over Taipei, daily life was normal. Each morning people hurried to work by foot, bus, car, motorcycle and scooter—many scooters. Work on the city's mass transit system would not begin until 1988. What I saw was an orderly society with low unemployment, rising living standards, busy weekend holidays and lively consumption in shops, restaurants and department stores.

Friends explained the situation had greatly changed from the 1950s. Then the government faced a possible invasion by the victorious communist armies and the widespread anger of many Taiwanese because of the brutal suppression of the 1947 rebellion. "In the Mainland, they had the 'Red Terror' and here we had the 'White Terror.' " was how one friend put it. In the 1960s and 1970s, however, the government had delivered average annual GDP growth of ten percent. In 1965, it opened the Kaohsiung Export Processing Zone, the first such zone in Asia; manufacturers received tax privileges provided they sold their products overseas. During the 1960s, Taiwan changed from a society based on agriculture to one based on industry and trade. It became one of Asia's 'four little dragons'.

By the 1970s, it had become the world's 14th largest trading land. Subsequently, many countries copied the Kaohsiung model, including China. Universal education had produced a literate and well-trained workforce. China Economic News, the magazine where I worked, concentrated on economics; we wrote little about politics, diplomacy or civil society. Our articles described the successes of Taiwan exporters and the need to stay ahead of foreign competitors by upgrading the standards of products and workers. We scarcely wrote about China; it had just started its reform program and set up four Special Economic Zones similar to the one in Kaohsiung. From a news point of view, we should have—but anything to do with China was sensitive. So the safest course for editors was not to write about it.

I asked Mainlander friends why martial law was still necessary. The island was prospering, with export markets around the world, and society was stable. "Yes, but the civil war is not over," they said. "Previously, the communists attacked us with military force. Now it is propaganda and infiltration. In the Mainland, the government made the mistake of allowing a multi-party system and a relatively free media. What was the outcome?"

The official line was that the Nationalists were the 'legal' government of China and the one in Beijing was 'illegal'. Foreigners found this puzzling. The civil war in the Mainland had ended in 1949, over thirty years before, and the communists occupied the whole country, except Taiwan, the smallest province. 'Illegal' after thirty-three years?

One evening I went to a cinema. Before the film, everyone stood up and sang the national anthem; I came to hear it so often that I know it by heart. During the anthem, we saw an official film about the products of Taiwan on the farms and the factories and scientists working diligently in laboratories. The island was white, while the Mainland was black; then the white of Taiwan spread over the Mainland, turning it white as well. We got the message. The media never mentioned concrete plans for an invasion, nor did anyone speak of them. They were military secrets. To me, it seemed completely impossible, given the huge superiority in numbers of the PLA compared to the Taiwan army. But you could never say that. This was the lifetime mission of Chiang Kai-shek. Even after he died in April 1975, it remained the goal of the government. It could not be questioned in public.

In 2009, we learned details of these invasion plans, after they were declassified and displayed at a museum in the Cihu Mausoleum, where Chiang is buried. On April 1, 1961, he set up Project Guoguang (國光計劃, Plan of National Glory), to supervise planning and preparation for the invasion. Chiang believed the Great Famine of 1959 to 1962, in which more than thirty million people died of starvation, had created the social instability needed for a successful invasion. But the US refused the help he asked for and desperately needed; without the Americans, he would fail. Four years later, he tried again, without asking the Americans. In June 1965, he told officers at the main Military Academy the invasion was imminent. Officers and soldiers in Quemoy, the front line closest to the Mainland, were told to draw up their last wills and testaments. But, again, the invasion never happened. In the early 1980s, nobody knew of these plans outside the government's elite. But, sometimes, if no one else was in earshot, friends criticized Chiang. "Why did he spend all these millions of dollars on the military and preparing to invade?" asked university student George Liu. "This was absurd. The government should spend the money on projects that benefit ordinary people."

When I visited Taiwan ten years later, George took me to one of the more than thirty villas around the island which Chiang used for himself, his family and guests, domestic and foreign.

He wanted to show the extravagance of the 'emperor'. This one was an hour's drive outside Taipei, up the side of a mountain; the villa was furnished modestly. What was distinctive was its location. The lawn in front looked down a steep mountain side and a river in the valley below.

"Chiang liked to sit in a chair on this lawn," said George. "The geography is exactly like that of Xikou, his hometown in Zhejiang Province. If he had drunk a little and closed his eyes, he could imagine he was still in Xikou. That was his dream. The problem of a dictator is that no one can question his decisions, however foolish and expensive." During the Chiang era, of course, we could not have visited these villas. During the democratic era, they have been open to the public, including his principal residence in Shilin, north Taipei.

Almost thirty years later, we learned of one of the most extreme consequences of this 'recovery' plan — the 'Black Bats'. Between 1952 and 1972, Taiwan pilots flew more than 800 surveillance missions over the Mainland in planes provided by the Central Intelligence Agency. It lost fifteen planes and one hundred forty-eight pilots, two-thirds of the total. The casualty rate was the highest of any of Taiwan's Special Forces. No wonder some called it the Black Widows Squadron. The aircraft had the latest electronic equipment and flew only at night, hence, the 'Black Bats' label. They collected valuable military intelligence, especially about bases, missile installations, air defense systems and the development of a nuclear bomb, which Taiwan shared with the US. It cost the US no servicemen, only the price of the planes. If they were shot down, it would be a 'China incident'; if an American pilot was shot down, it would be an 'international incident'.

This extraordinary operation finally came to light in November 2010, when a museum dedicated to the pilots opened on an air base in Hsinchu. The event was attended by the Defense Minister and General Ko Kuang-yue, former vice-chief of the Air Force. "Each time, they flew into a corridor of flame," Ko said. "Each mission was targeted by more than ten missiles, more than ten attacks by fighter planes and more than ten attacks of artillery fire. They came home and then flew another mission. They sacrificed themselves for this country. We must remember them forever."

Each plane carried nine to fourteen people, including pilots, mechanics, and radar and electronic specialists. They flew as far west as Qinghai and Xinjiang regions and as far north as Heilongjiang Province, on the Soviet border. One mission was to collect intelligence on the nuclear bomb Beijing was developing in the west. On June 1959, one flew over the Mainland for ten and a half hours at altitudes of between 19,000 to 21,000 meters. The PLA scrambled thirty-two planes; nine found the intruder and came within ten minutes of it but could not fly high enough to shoot it down.

All the pilots themselves were from the Mainland. "They wanted to go home. They wanted to fly," said a woman whose father was in the Air Force. "It was the mission of Chiang Kai-shek to recover the Mainland." At the opening ceremony of the museum, one former pilot, Li Chong-shan, said, "As soldiers, we could not fear. Taiwan was in a difficult situation. We had no money and no international status. We had to show this attitude and this courage of the soldiers and the government to earn the respect of our allies." When I lived in Taiwan in the early 1980s, I—and everyone else—knew nothing of this operation as it was top secret. One retired Taiwan diplomat said the Black Bats had two divisions. One was based in Taoyuan airport and flew the high-altitude missions all over China. The other was based in Hsinchu and used World War II propeller bombers such as B-17s to conduct low-flying missions over coastal areas; because they were slow, many were shot down. "These are all part of Cold War history," he said.

The most important day of the year was October 10, National Day. It memorializes the Xinhai Revolution of 1911, which overthrew the Qing Dynasty and established the Republic of China. In a letter, I described that day in 1981: "there was a huge military parade which passed outside our door. The troops goose-stepped almost in the style of the Nazis. I was most impressed — about 10,000 troops, tanks, personnel carriers, missiles, anti-aircraft guns, long-range artillery and militia from Kinmen (Quemoy) and Matsu. At 2:00 p.m., I joined the huge crowd outside the President's Palace for a display of gymnastics, dancing, acrobatics, music and a huge dragon dance. I was spellbound, especially by the children's dancing. In the evening, there was an hour-long display of fireworks above the banks of the Tamsui River running through the city. Apart from being crushed, I enjoyed that very much, like everyone else. Crowds were large but everyone was so pleasant and well mannered. If it were a Western city, half the crowd would be drunk or on drugs." The parade was the government's most important expression each year of its military prowess and its legitimacy as the ruler of China.

Another important day was November 12, the birthday of Dr Sun Yat-sen, the first President of the Republic of China and considered the 'Father of the Nation'. His photograph hung — and hangs — in government offices. When I was living in Taipei, it was a public holiday. By good fortune, it is also my birthday. I took this as a good omen. The government built a monumental Sun Yat-sen Memorial Hall; it attracts tens of thousands of visitors every year, including many from the Mainland. It overlooks a large open space, used by the public for Tai Chi, exercise, walking and relaxation.

The education system and the official narrative in the media and public events like National Day emphasized patriotism and love of China, its language, history and culture. But ordinary people knew little about what was happening on the other side of the Taiwan Strait. The media carefully controlled what was published about it; the government considered information part of the ongoing civil war. Those with better access were a limited number of specialists within the government and the academic community. They monitored what was going on better than anyone else in the world and sent reports to an elite in the military and the political leadership. For most Taiwan people I met, the Mainland was far away—a place they could not visit nor have any contact with.

One evening, my Taiwan friend Henry told a story: "It was in the 1960s. My family was watching a television broadcast by President Chiang Kai-shek. These were solemn events; everyone in our small dining room was quiet. In those days, there were no subtitles. My father understood Taiwanese and Japanese, but little Mandarin. The President spoke for about ten minutes. Then my father turned off the set. There was complete silence in the room. We stared at each other blankly.

'What did he say?' my father asked.

'Gas prices are going to increase,' I said as a guess.

'It might be sugar or bus fares,' my sister said.

Then everyone burst out laughing. "None of us had a clue. We had to wait until the next morning and read the paper to know find out what he said."

Henry liked to embellish his stories—but his meaning was clear enough. President Chiang had a thick accent of Ningbo, his native place, which many people found hard to understand. This was especially the case of Taiwanese of middle age and above who had not studied Mandarin at school. People who came from Shanghai and the provinces of Zhejiang and Jiangsu, close to Ningbo, could follow it more easily because their accents were similar. Like Chiang, many mainlanders did not speak Mandarin as their mother tongue and had to learn it. At home, they spoke the dialects of Shanghai, Guangdong, Sichuan and their native places.

His son Chiang Ching-kuo also had a Ningbo accent, but Henry said he could understand him. At the age of fifteen, his father had sent him to study in Moscow; he lived in the Soviet Union for twelve years and spoke and wrote fluent Russian. When he returned to China in 1937, his father ordered him to write an account of his life there; he feared his son had become a Communist Party member or sympathizer. Because Ching-kuo had used Mandarin so little in the Soviet Union, he had forgotten most of the characters. So he wrote the account in Russian; his father had a professor translate it into Chinese.

In May 1982, Hugh Sandeman, a visiting correspondent of the Economist magazine, told us a story about Sun Chen, a prominent economist. "Last year he was taking a shower early one morning. It was 6:00 a.m. The phone rang when Sun was half-asleep. The voice at the other end had a very thick accent, which he could barely make out. He was talking about a new job on offer. Sun concluded that it must be a wrong number and rang off. He went back into the shower. He wondered who might call him at that hour; what kind of accent did he have? Slowly it dawned on him that it must have been Number One (Chiang Ching-kuo—everyone knew he got up early in the morning). Sun rang back, apologized profusely and accepted the post."

The most famous story about Chiang's accent is a joke. In 1984, the National Assembly was meeting in Taipei. Chiang was to announce his choice as vice-president. Just a few minutes before his speech, his secretary still did not know the name of the nominee and was becoming anxious. He looked everywhere for his boss and finally found him in the men's room. He banged on the door and asked for the name. Chiang said, "你等一會兒", "Ni deng yihuir ("Please wait a moment.") The secretary took him to mean Lee Teng-hui, the person he actually chose. The point of this story was that Chiang's staff sometimes did not know exactly what their boss meant. To make the joke better, Lee was a surprise choice.

His brother, Chiang Wei-kuo, spoke Mandarin better. He had a formal education in China and studied physics at Suzhou University. I met him once at a wedding in Taipei in April 1982; he spoke very clearly. The problem was not restricted to leaders in Taiwan. Many revolutionary leaders in the Mainland had limited formal schooling. Their education was guerilla warfare and underground organizing. Mao Zedong had a thick Hunan accent, and Deng Xiaoping a thick Sichuan accent. When Deng was feeling humorous, he used to tell foreign journalists in Beijing that some spoke Mandarin better than he. I wondered how many policy mistakes resulted from these accents. Advisers and officials of these veteran leaders were frightened of them. If they did not understand exactly what they heard, they should have asked for a repetition—but sometimes they did not dare, and the leader was not advised of his mistake.

Like the rest of the media, we at the magazine had to be extra careful in writing about the 'Royal Family'. We could only use official descriptions of them and their activities, with no comment by others or speculation of our own. When I arrived, the President was Chiang Ching-kuo, son of Chiang Kai-shek. Like his father, he was an ever-present in the newspapers and on television. He was a more 'modern' leader. On weekends, he used to visit towns and villages around Taiwan wearing casual clothes and a baseball cap—something his father would never have done. He talked to the local people, ate snacks and drank the local specialty juices and wines. Later I learned he never told his chauffeur in advance where he planned to go for these weekend trips. It was his attempt to avoid an 'official visit' in which every person and remark are choreographed in advance. Such visits, Chiang believed, taught him nothing because people were instructed to say what he wanted to hear.

It was, I think, his modest attempt to democratize a system that was highly centralized. Like his father, he governed under the 1947 constitution. In November that year, an election was held across most of China—but not Taiwan—that chose 3,000 deputies; they took office in March 1948. When the Nationalist government moved to Taiwan in 1949, about half the deputies went with it. Since the government could not hold elections again in the Mainland, those elected in 1947 remained in their seats. When one died, he was replaced by someone chosen from natives of the same province who were resident in Taiwan. Local people mockingly called these deputies "10,000-year representatives" (萬年代表). Sick and elderly ones were brought to sessions in wheelchairs or even on beds. Their tenure finally ended on December 1991, under reforms implemented by Lee Teng-hui, Chiang's successor. The term in office lasted forty-three years and 278 days! A Taiwan journalist told me he often went to interview deputies at their annual meeting. He found the one who represented the Uighurs in the far west of China, distinctive because he had Turkic features and not those of a Han Chinese. The journalist addressed him in Mandarin but discovered that he could not speak it. The man lived in Istanbul and only came to Taipei for the annual meetings. A descendant of a representative elected in 1947, he spoke several languages—but not Chinese

Chiang Ching-kuo was best known among Taiwan people

for the 'Ten Major Projects' he undertook as Prime Minister in 1974, costing NT$300 billion, and completed by 1979. They were three industrial projects, one power plant and six transport projects, including a North-South freeway, electrification of the main West Coast railway and the Chiang Kai-shek International Airport. These were popular with the public because they greatly facilitated their daily life. But, as a loyal son, Chiang could not abandon his father's mission of recovering the Mainland. But, my Taiwan friends told me, his strategy was not to invade but rather to support a potential uprising that might occur in the Mainland. So spending for possible offensive operations could be greatly curtailed.

The official media presented Chiang as active and hard-working, especially on the economy. How little we knew. Later we learned that, in the early 1980s, his health was deteriorating. The diabetes he had inherited from his mother was so serious that two doctors were on 24-hour standby at his house to monitor his blood sugar. The trips to the countryside made it worse. Instead of following the strict dietary advice of his doctors, he ate whatever he liked, including ice cream, a substance banned because of its high sugar content. He had pain in his legs and needed sedation to sleep. By the end of 1983, he could barely walk. His home, called Seven Seas, become his office; he barely used the Presidential Palace in downtown Taipei. We at the United Daily News and the general public knew nothing about any of this. Western leaders were the same—French President Francois Mitterrand died in 1996 of prostate cancer one year after leaving office; he had successfully concealed it from the public throughout his presidency from 1981 to 1995.

We knew next to nothing about Chiang's family. Friends told me he had a wife and children but there was little official information about them. His wife never appeared in public. The most dramatic suggestion I heard from a friend was that his wife was a member of the family of Nicholas II, last Tsar of Russia, who was killed by the Bolsheviks on July 17, 1918. It was a good guess. We later learned that she, Faina, was from Belarus and had met Chiang in 1933 in the factory where both were working in Yekaterinburg in the center of Russia. We also learned she stayed out of the public eye in Taiwan in part because she preferred it that way and in part because a Russian wife might raise suspicions Chiang had links to the Soviet Union and the Communist Party.

We knew more about Song Mei-ling, the widow of Chiang Kai-shek. Unlike Faina, she enjoyed the public spotlight. After her husband's death, she moved to the United States, where the family had a 14.6-hectare estate in Nassau County, New York. She only returned to Taiwan three times. She was not Ching-kuo's mother—that was Chiang Kai-shek's first wife, who was killed by a Japanese air raid in her hometown of Xikou in December 1939. Most Taiwan people took Madame Song's move to the US to mean she had lost the great political influence she had enjoyed with her husband. As a Chinese saying goes, there is no room for two tigers on the same mountain.

Taiwan friends told me President Chiang Kai-shek lived in a house in Shilin, north of Taipei, but it was a military area they could not visit. We had to wait until January 2011 until it was open to the public. The main entrance leads into a sumptuous garden, with lawns, pools, many different trees and Chinese pavilions. Walk along the path, turn left and you see a modest two-story western-style home. My first thought was that it was too small for the 'Emperor' of China. Presumably, Chiang only expected to spend a few years there before returning to the Mainland. Guides explained Chiang died in April 1975 and his wife, Song Mei-ling, lived until October 2003, when she died at the age of 105. "She came back to Taiwan three times after her husband's death and used to stay here," one said. "After she died, the building passed to the Taipei city government, which renovated it before opening it to the public."

Before 1945, it had been the site of the Shilin Horticultural Experimental Station built in 1908; it was the foundation of the beautiful garden. In the 1950s, the government took over the building, added a second floor and Chiang and his wife moved in. It had the benefit of being a long way from the road and easy to defend. In the surrounding area were built homes of military officers. The ground floor has several living rooms and a banquet hall with room for sixteen; the second floor has separate studies for Chiang and his wife, his office, a dining room and bedrooms. Originally, the two slept in two beds in the same room. After Chiang's health deteriorated late in life, he moved to another bedroom; that was where he died. "On the evening of his death, Taiwan was hit by a powerful storm," the guide said. This was a sign of the importance of his passing. She said Chiang and his wife had different schedules—Chiang got up early, washed and did exercises. Each day he meditated, read the Bible and prayed. He liked to wear traditional Chinese gowns or military uniforms, but rarely Western suits.

Madame Song liked to paint and read books. She slept late and got up late. After she moved to Taiwan, she invited famous painters to the house to teach her; some of her paintings are hanging on the walls. She and her husband liked to watch films in the house. Having studied in the US for nine years, including at Wellesley College, she spoke flawless England and liked American films. In a garage near the entrance is a seven-seat Cadillac she used from 1988 to 2004. Among the items on the ground floor was an 'Anti-Communist Victory' chess game designed by one of his staff. In the grounds is a Victory Chapel built in 1950, where Chiang and his wife worshipped every Sunday, along with senior KMT generals. President Dwight D. Eisenhower and then Vice-President Richard Nixon also attended services there.

Even fifty years after his death, the name of Chiang Kai-shek arouses powerful and conflicting emotions among Taiwan people. Those who belong to his Kuomintang Party said that, without him, the PLA would have taken over the island, as it did the rest of China. So his rule saved Taiwan and laid the basis for its remarkable economic prosperity today. Many native Taiwan people see him differently. "He was a bandit," said a retired teacher. "He and the people who came with him from the Mainland treated Taiwan like their personal fiefdom. He had thirty-seven villas around the island for his personal use. They are open to the public now. We hold him responsible for the killings after the February 28 (1947) rebellion and the White Terror that followed."

Chiang Ching-kuo gave more space than his father to those who opposed him. They could not form a political party nor join the government but could run as independents in elections. Taiwan journalists could not interview them nor publish what they said, but foreign journalists could. Unsure of the protocol, I contacted foreign reporters in Taipei. Most were Americans; some had been with their country's military before relations were broken with Washington in 1979 and stayed on after their army left. They were not subject to the restrictions of those working for Taiwan media; they liked to tell jokes about the Chiang family and other members of the ruling elite. They had the privilege of meeting members of the opposition.

For these people, a foreign journalist was important since his newspaper was willing to publish their views, which the Taiwan media could not. At my request, an American reporter took me to meet one of them. I did not know what to expect. The man lived in a fourth-floor flat of a Taipei apartment building. At the entrance was a man with a black shirt and black trousers, smoking a cigarette. "That is the plainclothes policeman," the reporter said. "They watch who goes in and out but usually do not interfere."

The dissident turned out to be a well-informed man in his forties, a schoolteacher, who had studied in the US and returned to Taiwan to continue the 'struggle'. He welcomed us with green tea and pineapple cakes, a Taiwan specialty. His apartment was small and well furnished; it was lined with books.

"The system of government here is completely out-of-date," he said. "These members of the legislature were chosen in an election in the Mainland in 1947. What right do they have to represent the people of Taiwan in the 1980s? It is ridiculous. We need a democratic system that reflects the will of Taiwan people. We are well educated and know how the world works." He spoke forcefully and without apparent anxiety. "And why should we want to recover the Mainland after so many years? They have their own system there and we have ours. We should leave each other alone and not attack each other. We need foreign governments, especially the United States, to put pressure on the Kuomintang to make these changes." He had a lot more to say and the American reporter and I took copious notes.

As we walked out of the building, he waved at the smoking policeman. "The dissident has a reasonable case," I said. "Twenty years ago, he would have been locked up," my friend replied. "But Taiwan has moved on. The government is willing to tolerate such criticism now. It needs to retain the goodwill of the US government, which pays attention to democratic rights." In addition, thousands of Taiwan people had studied in the West and knew how the governments of their countries worked. The system based on the 1947 election was not sustainable. Everyone called these dissidents 'Dang Wai', meaning 'Outside the Party, that is, outside the Kuomintang. Over the years that followed, I met several of them. One told me, "We like meeting foreigners like you. It is very relaxing. You know so little and ask easy questions."

On September 28, 1986, at the Grand Hotel in Taipei, eighteen organizing members founded the Democratic Progressive Party (DPP). A total of one hundred thirty-two people joined. The party was 'illegal', because martial law was still in force and banned opposition parties. But they set it up because they knew Chiang Ching-kuo would tolerate it; his father would not have done so. Those early members were family members, defense lawyers of political prisoners and intellectuals who had spent time abroad. Their platform was democracy and freedom of speech, press, assembly and association. No one at the meeting imagined that, just fourteen years later, the Taiwan people would elect a DPP president.

Like the vast majority of the Taiwan public, I had no idea how ill Chiang Ching-kuo was, nor that he was in a hurry. As the son of the 'Emperor', he was the only one with the authority to change the system under which his father had governed Taiwan since 1949. His most important decision was to abolish martial law, on July 15, 1987, after thirty-eight years. Lifting the ban permitted the formation of opposition political parties for the first time, and establishment of media not controlled by the government or the Kuomintang. It was a milestone toward the creation of a free and democratic society. We did not know — but he probably did — that he had only six more months to live.

In October that year, he announced another major change — residents of Taiwan were permitted to visit the Mainland to visit their families, for the first time in thirty-eight years. This was especially important for those who had arrived in 1949 as adults and feared that they would never see their relatives again. Later, I met several who had made the trip. They described it as emotional and traumatic. I found two different reactions. Those who had left family members and knew them personally were delighted to see again their parents, brothers and sisters, cousins, neighbors and classmates.

The other group were the children of these people. They had been born in Taiwan and had no personal knowledge of the relatives they went to see. As filial children, they accompanied their parents on the trip. For them, the visit was a great shock — to see the difference in living conditions, appearance and thinking between them and their relatives. They did not have the personal empathy to offset the shock. This was particularly the case of those who went to small towns and rural areas poorer than the cities where the economy was improving. "One shock was the amount of money we had to spend," said a salesman in his thirties who went with his mother to her hometown in Jiangsu. "Everyone said Taiwan was rich and we had to give residents gifts like radios, televisions, bicycles and watches. After we arrived, the news spread around the village and many people appeared, asking for items. We did not know most of them, even my mother did not know. I estimate the whole visit cost us $10,000. My mother wants to go again, but I do not."

What struck everyone was the enormous gap in outlook and behavior between them and their mainland relatives after forty years of separation. The two societies had developed in opposite directions and lived in different universes.

Let us close this chapter with two letters I wrote in February 1982 and the autumn of 1983 to friends in Britain that try to capture the atmosphere of those two years.

February 1982: "There are many good points to living here,

an independent Chinese republic and not a hybrid like Hong Kong. Here we whites are truly foreigners, with no privileges except being treated with good manners. The transformation of this island is no less than extraordinary than that of Hong Kong: thirty-seven years ago, an agricultural backwater of China just released from fifty years of Japanese rule. Now it is a highly industrialized and overcrowded place that is home to the second government of China. An estimated two million people escaped here in 1949 and still occupy most of the senior positions in government and the military. The economic power rests for the most part with the 15 million native Taiwanese. The outlook of the two is different, especially among the older generation. The latter look upon this island as home, for good or ill, the former as a temporary home, either before they recover the Mainland or a second flight from the 'bandits' to the US, Canada or Australia. Because the government here was defeated, it has gone over backwards to preserve and cultivate its Chinese-ness, to stake its claim as the real government. For a foreigner, this is a great good fortune."

Autumn 1983: "Life in Taiwan is as absorbing as I hoped it would be — less the stabbing (Chapter1). It is a semi-secret society, less open than Hong Kong or Europe but much more so than the communist countries. Each morning's paper is a parody. It is full of detailed analysis and news of no importance in the United States, while right here, and even more so over the water, things of momentous significance are going on, but unreported. News about China is tightly controlled. Still, information is available, and not too far beneath the surface. My conversations with people keep returning to the years 1945-49 — How could Chiang Kai-shek lose? Could it have happened differently? What would have happened to China if he had held power?

"The civil war is unfinished. The communists have won

the territorial and diplomatic battles, but the economic and technological battle has been won handsomely by this side. The Republic of China does not need to negotiate, not yet for some while anyway. So the significant news in China these days in my view is its attempt to catch up with Taiwan. The whole country cannot do it obviously but some areas can—like Shenzhen, the Xiamen Special Economic Zones and Shanghai. They are the models for the future of both here and Hong Kong/Macau. The more poetical among the Chinese here see that: 'They have the land and the resources, largely untapped. We have the knowhow and the manpower to exploit it. But, because Taiwan is too small and too much a colony of the US, we lose eighty percent of our best students overseas, especially to the US. Most of them would rather go to China if they could. We need each other.' "

In the chapters that follow, we will find out which of these observations proved to be more accurate and which were not.

5

THE PRESBYTERIAN CHURCH AND THE TAIWANESE LANGUAGE

I was walking through the National Museum of Taiwan History, in Tainan, capital of the island for two hundred years until 1887, in the southwest. It was a spacious and well-appointed building, with space dedicated to the different periods in Taiwan's complicated history. There were many images and detailed explanations—what a museum ought to be. To my surprise, I came to a room dedicated to western missionaries, many of them Presbyterian. The Presbyterian Church of Taiwan (PCT) was established on June 6, 1865. It is the same church to which my grandfather Frederick belonged; he was a missionary in Liaoning, northeast China, from 1897 to 1942. The room had a photograph of each missionary and details of his home country, his life and work in Taiwan and his contribution to its people. There was a recorder with the favorite hymn of each missionary; at the click of a button, you could hear it sung in Taiwanese, Mandarin or English.

I was overwhelmed. Never had I seen in a foreign land such an exhibition of love and respect toward the missionaries. In Taiwan, they have made a major contribution to the health, education, religion and social welfare in an island that was in the 19th Century a poor and backward region of China. The

PCT established many firsts in Taiwan—the first modern school, including the first school for girls, the blind and the deaf, the first western hospital, care for leprosy patients and the first printing press in Taiwan. I was so overwhelmed that I later wrote a message of gratitude to the director of the museum; I praised him for the objectivity and detail of the exhibits. He graciously acknowledged the message.

Among the names in the exhibition, one jumped out—George Leslie Mackay. Cycling through central Taipei, I often passed the Mackay Memorial Hospital, an imposing building with fifteen stories and 1,200 beds. His Chinese name is Ma Jie—everyone in Taiwan knew him. Born in Ontario, Canada, on March 21, 1844, he studied theology in Toronto and Edinburgh; he also studied dentistry in Toronto and New York. In December 1871, he arrived in Taiwan; his first challenge was to master Taiwanese, no simple task. To do this, he avoided the company of foreigners as much as possible. He made friends with a dozen shepherd boys; after five months, he was able to preach in Taiwanese. He also learned Chinese characters and, in 1875, published an English-Chinese dictionary. Discovering that many people suffered from rotten teeth, he used his medical knowledge to remove them—this made him very popular.

At that time, the unwritten rule among western missionaries in China was that they marry Caucasian women, usually from the same religious and missionary milieu. Instead, Mackay chose a Chinese girl from a poor local family who had converted. In 1880, he founded the Mackay Clinic in Tamsui north of Taipei. It was the first western hospital in the northern part of Taiwan. He combined medicine and evangelism. This is what the hospital website says about him: "during his twenty years in Taiwan, he received help from many foreign doctors. They treated patients suffering from a host of diseases, including malaria, which was a significant problem at that time.

Besides treating patients, Dr MacKay often preached and took teams of Taiwanese Christians with him on his medical and evangelistic tours in northern Taiwan. With the Bible in one hand and dental forceps in the other, he defied mountains, rivers and jungle overgrowth to do medical evangelism. Although practicing medicine and evangelizing Taiwan were very difficult work at that time, Dr MacKay endured for more than thirty years. During this time, he not only pulled more than 20,000 teeth, but also proclaimed the gospel to different people around the island," it said. He died on June 2, 1901, of throat cancer, at the age of fifty-eight. During his life, he established sixty churches and the Oxford College in Tamsui to train Taiwanese evangelists. In 1912, the Mackay Memorial Hospital was moved to the capital Taipei.

This is how the *Stories of Chinese Christianity* described him: "George Mackay left behind a thriving church of sixty congregations led by Chinese and Aboriginal preachers; Oxford College, which became what is now Aletheia University and the Taiwan Seminary; the Tamkang Girls School; the Tamkang Middle School (now High School), of which Mackay's son George was appointed principal; Mackay Hospital and a strong presence of the Canadian Presbyterian mission. This later became the North Taiwan Presbytery and later merged with the southern presbytery to become the Taiwan Presbyterian Church. He had greatly enhanced the lives of the women whom his ministry touched, and set a pattern of treating women with respect for later generations. For these and other reasons, George Leslie Mackay has been hailed as one of the greatest missionaries to China in the nineteenth century." The PCT was a pioneer in establishing western medical hospitals and modern schools in Taiwan, including for women. In July 1970, the Mackay Memorial

Hospital set up the Mackay Nursing College.

Another thing I learned from the exhibition was that Presbyterian missionaries created a Romanized script for the Taiwanese language. As one church member told me, this came about after the missionaries gave out Bibles in Chinese characters to their congregations but almost none of them could read it. Knowledge of characters was confined to a small class of officials, wealthy people and intelligentsia. So the missionaries, including Mackay, created a system to read the language using Roman letters. An illiterate person needed years to learn written Chinese, but he could grasp this system of twenty-six letters and a few diacritical and tonal marks in a matter of months. In 1885, the PCT published the island's first newspaper, the Tai-oan Kau-hoe Kong-po (Taiwan Church News) using this script. It was published for nearly a century, until 1969. I went to the National Museum of Taiwan Literature, also in Tainan. By a stroke of good fortune, on that day it had an exhibition on the Taiwanese language. I met a middle-aged museum official, named Lin, who was a devotee of the language. He showed me letters, newspapers, magazines, books and a Bible written in the language. He explained it was being used in schools to teach children (in 2016). The two exhibitions opened my eyes. Learning Mandarin in Taipei, I had only seen material written in Chinese characters. I had, of course, heard a great deal of Taiwanese spoken but not seen it in written form. As our discussions continued, Mr Lin became increasingly angry. "This might have been one of the official languages of Taiwan," he said. "But it is not, first because of the Japanese and later because of the Kuomintang."

Japan ruled Taiwan from 1895 to 1945 and made Japanese the official language in the government, the schools and business. It discouraged the use of Taiwanese. This is how the official

PCT history describes this period: "There were major conflicts between the PCT and the Japanese colonial government, especially in education. During the period of making Taiwan people 'subjects of the Emperor' (kominka), the church faced many restrictions in its services and education." The conflicts were less severe between 1895 and 1931, when other Protestant denominations arrived to do evangelical work in Taiwan. But, after Japan occupied Manchuria in 1931, the conflict sharpened as Tokyo's relations with western countries deteriorated.

The colonial government considered the PCT disloyal, since it was a champion of the Taiwanese people and language. The church was forced to hold at least one service a week in Japanese, sing the Japanese national anthem and pray for soldiers who had died. The PCT seminary and girls' schools were not allowed to use Taiwanese; teachers who did not speak Japanese were dismissed and foreign teachers were expelled from Taiwan. In the fourteen years between 1931 and 1945, the Japanese policy, in Taiwan as in Korea, was kominka (皇民化), to make Taiwan people like those in Japan and Japanese the standard language. It wanted them to wear Japanese clothing and adopt Japanese names. It had done the same in Okinawa, as I had learned from Tomi, my roommate in Taipei. The use of the Taiwanese language was severely restricted.

Mr Lin said when the Kuomintang took over in 1945, they followed the same language policy as the colonial government, with Mandarin replacing Japanese. "They banned Taiwanese in the schools, the media and government. We could not publish books in the Taiwanese language." The official rationale was that, since it was the government of all China, not only Taiwan, it must therefore use the national language, in preparation for the day when the country was reunited.

In addition, it argued, while the native language of the

majority was Taiwanese, people in the island spoke many forms of Chinese. Not all mainlanders spoke Mandarin; many used their own dialects, such as from Shanghai, Guangdong, Shandong and Sichuan, or Hakka. It was necessary to have Mandarin as the common language. Many mainlanders, including President Chiang Kai-shek, also had to learn it.

It was only after the end of martial law in July 1987 that the restrictions began to be eased, said Mr Lin. "After a president from the Democratic Progressive Party took power in 2000, the status of Taiwanese greatly improved and it was used on radio and television and taught in schools." But, he said bitterly, it was too late. "Even my Taiwanese friends prefer to use Mandarin, especially for written communications and in official forums. They have grown too comfortable with it. The ban on Taiwanese lasted too long. We have lost."

Later I visited a Presbyterian church in Taipei and was given a Biblical leaflet written in both Chinese characters and Romanized Taiwanese. I showed it to Taiwanese friends and asked them to read it. They blinked and did not know what to say. Most said that they could not because they were unfamiliar with the script. One said if I gave him a few weeks he would be able to read it. So Mr Lin was correct. I concluded that outside the 220,000 members of the PCT, few Taiwan people could read the script.

An exhibit on the Taiwan Church News history eloquently told the story of the language. In 1884, a Scottish Presbyterian missionary named Thomas Barclay set up a machine shop. In June the next year, he printed the first issue of Taiwan Church News, the first printed newspaper in the island. It used the Taiwan written language. In 1913, the press produced more than 700,000 pages, mostly in the Taiwanese language. In 1915, the newspaper had a circulation of 1,600. In the 1942, the Japanese government closed the newspaper. After 1945, it resumed publication. But, in 1969, the Kuomintang government banned it from using Taiwanese and ordered it to use Chinese characters, which it has done since then. In 1987, the government seized an entire print run of 6,700 copies, because it discussed the February 28, 1947, incident—a forbidden topic. Since 1991, after the ban was lifted, it has continued to use characters, with a small section using Taiwanese and other native languages.

Later I met someone more radical than Mr Lin. It was during a visit to the Taipei 2-28 Memorial Museum in the city center, opposite the Presidential Palace; we mentioned it in Chapter Two. Such a museum was, of course, unimaginable during the martial law period. In 1995, President Lee Teng-hui offered an apology on behalf of the government to the victims of the White Terror. The museum opened on February 28, 1997, the 50th anniversary of the event. After I entered, a man stepped forward and said in Mandarin, "Would you like a tour guide?" I said I would.

"Fine, but I will only speak in Taiwanese or Japanese, not Mandarin, the language of the occupier," he said. Fortunately, since we had lived in Tokyo for nearly four years, we had a reasonable understanding of Japanese. That, plus the characters on the exhibits, made it possible to understand the guide; he was as passionate as Mr Lin about Taiwanese and he gave me a leaflet in Japanese on the 2-28 incident. The tour was startling, especially to someone with no detailed understanding of the rebellion and the White Terror that followed. The rooms gave details of those killed during the White Terror, including photographs and biographies; many were students, lawyers, doctors and other members of the island's elite. The exhibits made the killings and arrests vivid and tragic. The guide emphasised the arbitrary nature of the repression, with the security forces arresting and imprisoning people on suspicion and without due process.

Having lived in Taiwan under martial law when the rule of Chiang Kai-shek could not be questioned, I found it astonishing that a public museum could describe in such detail killings for which Chiang was ultimately responsible. After thanking our guide, I walked outside into the sunlight of the park. On the other side of a wide avenue was the palace where President Chiang had ruled Taiwan with an iron fist from 1949 until his death in 1975. Seeing the two buildings facing each other in the center of the city left me in a state of shock.

But a sense of revenge is not the mission of the museum. This was what the Taiwan Ministry of Culture says about it: "the museum's mission is to provide a public, historical account of the 2-28 Incident and to console the family members of victims of the incident. It is to help all people in Taiwan better understand the 2-28 Incident, and transform the suffering associated with the incident into a source of strength. With this goal in mind, the Museum hopes to renew the soul of Taiwan and create a harmonious society through love and forgiveness. The museum also hopes to promote ethnic harmony and sharing in society, and the sound development of culture."

Its aim was similar to that of the Truth and Reconciliation Commission set up in South Africa in 1996 after the end of apartheid. The Commission invited the victims of human rights abuses and those who committed them to appear and explain what had happened. It set up a register of reconciliation so ordinary people could express remorse for what they had done. They could request amnesty from civil and criminal prosecution. The commission could grant this as long as the crimes were politically motivated, proportionate and the person made full disclosure.

While I lived in Taiwan from 1981 to 1983, I knew little of the PCT and the Taiwanese language. My world consisted of

Mandarin, official media and Chinese-speaking friends; none belonged to the PCT. Its membership, about 200,000 members, was a fraction of the total population. Many were Aborigines, descendants of the inhabitants of Taiwan before the arrival of the Han Chinese from the 17th Century; most lived in remote, mountainous areas. The first PCT minister who came to my attention was Reverend Kao Chun-ming, secretary-general of the church since 1970. He was arrested on April 24, 1980, for helping those involved in a protest in Kaohsiung in 1979 and sentenced to seven years in prison. International church groups and the US considered him a victim of political persecution for speaking out against human rights violations and the lack of democracy on Taiwan. American journalists in Taiwan told me about his case and showed me articles in the US media about him. Probably as a result of international pressure, he was released on parole on August 15, 1984.

Taiwan friends explained that, during the period of martial law, the PCT was the most organized opposition to the Kuomintang. It was able to do this because of its nationwide network of congregations, deep roots in society and its use in church of Taiwanese, one of the rare public spaces where this was possible. Martial law did not mean restrictions on religion. The government boasted that freedom of religion was one of the things that distinguished it from the Mainland. President Chiang Kai-shek and his family were Methodists and worshipped at the Chapel of Victory at their residence each weekend. Mindful of US sensitivities, the government had to be careful in handling Christian churches.

In 1971, Taiwan was expelled from the United Nations and replaced by the People's Republic of China. Its place in the world was uncertain. In light of this, the PCT, under the leadership of Revered Kao, released three important statements. On December

29, 1971, it issued the Statement of Our National Fate by the Presbyterian Church in Taiwan. "We oppose any powerful nation disregarding the rights and wishes of 15 million people and making unilateral decisions to their own advantage, because God ordained, and the United Nations Charter has affirmed, that every people has the right to determine its own destiny... We do not wish to be governed by Peiping (Beijing)... We earnestly request that, within the Taiwan area, the government hold elections of all representatives to the highest government bodies to succeed the present representatives who were elected twenty-five years ago on the Mainland."

Then, in November 1975, it issued a second statement that also called for political reformation and a truly democratic government. The statement protested against the confiscation earlier that year of Bibles printed in the Taiwanese language. After negotiations, they were returned. "We urge that the freedom to continue to publish and distribute the Bible in any language be guaranteed." The third statement on August 16, 1977, was the most dramatic. "We insist the future of Taiwan shall be determined by the seventeen million people who live there... To achieve our goal of independence and freedom for the people of Taiwan in this critical international situation, we urge our government to face reality and to take effective measures whereby Taiwan may become a new and independent country." Under martial law, who dared to call for an independent Taiwan? Reverend Kao was one of many members of the PCT involved in the opposition movement during the 1980s.

In the early 2000s, I had the opportunity to interview two leaders of the PCT in their modest office off Roosevelt Road in central Taipei. On the walls were photographs of the early Presbyterian missionaries, with explanations in English, Chinese and Taiwanese script. The two spoke with force and determination, repeating the themes of the three statements in the 1970s. "We fought for the Taiwanese people against the Japanese, the Kuomintang and now the communists," one said. "It is the people of Taiwan alone who can decide our future. We have no relations with Mainland China and do not wish to be ruled by them." Such a democratic choice was in accord with the Charter of the United Nations and the will of God, he said. I was impressed by the strength of their faith and convictions.

One devout member of the church was Lee Teng-hui, who became President on the death of Chiang Ching-kuo in January 1988 and held the post for the next twelve years. How much did his church and religion influence his actions as president?

6

Civil Society Blossoms after Martial Law

The abolition of martial law in July 1987 led to a blossoming of civil society. For nearly forty years after its arrival in 1949, the KMT government strived to control all aspects of society. It allowed only one political party and there was no media it did not control. Its rationale was that too much freedom had allowed the Communists to take power. While it permitted freedom of religion, in 1949 it set up the Buddhist Association of the Republic of China to control and supervise the practice of Buddhism on the island. By the 1980s, Taiwan's society and economy had changed so much that such controls were no longer tenable. The level of education was high. Tens of thousands of Taiwan people had worked and studied abroad, especially in the United States. There they saw the essential role NGOs played in American society, education, sports, social welfare and politics. By 1987, the KMT could no longer keep the lid on the box. After martial law ended, the energy inside the box burst out—Taiwan people were able to express their talents and energy.

In the elections for the Legislative Yuan in January 2020, the four largest parties received 86 percent of the votes—but a total of 46 political parties took part. Once I visited a party whose platform was to make Taiwan the 51st state of the US—innovative but improbable. There were even two Communist parties. Today the island accredits more than 40,000 non-governmental organisations; about 2,000 are affiliated with international NGOs or have links to associations abroad. The government encourages foreign NGOs to set up offices on the island. Those which did so in 2022 included US Freedom House, the Czech Republic's European Values Center for Security Policy, Spain's Safeguard Defenders, and Japan's Safeguard Defenders. The Ministry of Foreign Affairs has a Department of NGO International Relations and the ministry partners with NGOs on behalf of the executive branch. On its website, the Ministry said: "civil society today plays a key role in ensuring good governance and in enabling Taiwan to exert its soft power in the international arena. Indeed, NGOs have raised Taiwan's profile by engaging in various international cooperation projects closely aligned with the UN Millennium Development Goals. These include providing international humanitarian, medical assistance, eradicating poverty and disease, promoting democracy and human rights and environmental sustainability." In the absence of official relations with most countries, Taiwan must use NGOs to project soft power abroad.

NGOs were born out of religious movements and alumni, academics, professional and community associations. They collect and sort rubbish, they clean beaches and mountain trails, they care for the sick, the old and the infirm, they arrange sports events, plays, concerts, book talks, art shows and academic events and organize study and sports tours abroad. They carry out humanitarian missions in foreign countries; one runs a bone marrow bank. They also campaign for social and political rights and protest when they think the government has made a mistake.

In religion, Taiwanese are eclectic. A 2021 survey by Academia Sinica found the three biggest religions to be traditional folk religions, 27.9 percent, Buddhists 19.8 percent, and Taoist 18.7

percent. In addition, there are Protestants, Catholics, Mormons, Muslims, Bahai, Jews and many others. More than half of those surveyed said they practiced several religions, especially Buddhism and Taoism.

Among the groups to take advantage of the new freedoms after July 1987 were four large Buddhist movements—the Tzu Chi Foundation, Fo Guang Shan (the Mountain of the Shining Buddha), Dharma Drum Mountain and Chung Tai Shan. They were able to establish mass movements, raise large amounts of money from the public and communicate with them through radio, television and new channels made possible by the internet and information technology. The prosperity of Taiwan had created a growing and well educated middle class; its members responded with passion and energy to the appeal of the movements and took part in their programs. The government encouraged them, especially in charity, education, disaster relief and environmentalism; they reduced the obligations of the government in these areas and helped to maintain social stability. They also helped to soften the conflict between the Mainlander and Taiwanese; in Buddhism, of course, there is no such distinction, as there is none between Chinese and foreigners.

In terms of numbers and operations, the largest NGO in Taiwan, and in the Chinese-speaking world, is the Tzu Chi Foundation. It was founded in 1966 by Master Cheng Yen, a nun. It has 10 million members around the world, half of them in Taiwan. Of the ten million, about two million are volunteers, giving their time and expertise free of charge. For the first 20 years, it concentrated its charity at home. After 1987, it was able to expand abroad. Its 2021 annual report said that it had volunteers in sixty-six countries and regions. It has provided charity in one hundred twenty-eight countries, helped to build 22,000 'Great Love' homes and 246 schools in sixteen countries and regions. It has held 17,400 free medical clinics that served 3.55 million people. It has distributed 1.25 million blankets to victims of natural disasters in forty-four countries and 147,000 metric tons of rice in nineteen countries. During the Covid-19 pandemic, it provided more than 50.7 million face masks, personal protection suits and other items required by medical staff and ordinary people in ninety-seven countries and regions. These are astonishing statistics for an NGO based in a land of 23 million people, which was expelled from the United Nations in 1971; as of August 2023, it had diplomatic relations with only 12 countries that are members of the United Nations, and with the Holy See.

As I mentioned in the Foreword, I had the good fortune to spend a year with the members of the Foundation, writing a book about its history. It was unforgettable. Their headquarters is the "Abode of Still Thoughts", a modest grey building in Tang dynasty style in a rural area south of Hualien, on the east coast of Taiwan. Master Cheng Yen lives there with her community of nuns; they cultivate the land and make items which they sell for their daily living. The setting is dramatic. In front is the Pacific Ocean, its waves loud and powerful. Behind is the Central Mountain Range that runs through the middle of the island. The area has regular earthquakes. All this gives a sense of fragility of human and natural life. Master Cheng Yen likes to say "人生無常" — "rensheng wuchang", nothing in life is normal. Be prepared for anything — including death or injury. Then the rural silence around the Abode is broken by the crashing sound of fighter jets from a nearby air base on practice runs. What is normal? When I visited the Abode, I saw the stream of disciples from Taiwan and around the world; they report their charity projects to Master Cheng Yen, who guides and encourages them. In the midst of this fragility and uncertainty, man can do good and improve the lot of his fellow human beings — that was the message.

There are many reasons for the success of the foundation. One is that it has 'localized'. The pioneer members in a country are Taiwanese, usually in business or professionals; they inspire local people to join them and expand the work. The second is the economic success of Taiwan itself. It has produced many people of goodwill and sufficient wealth who are able to make regular financial contributions and give their time free of charge. The third is Tzu Chi's success in remaining neutral, non-political and non-aligned, allowing it to work in Islamic, Christian and Hindu countries and Mainland China. While it is Buddhist, it does not proselytize; this is an important precondition to work in many countries.

The Foundation funds its many projects out of donations from its members, individual and corporate. Annual donations total more than $300 million. The majority of donors are individuals; many, including my wife and me, pay a fixed amount per month. Some donations are large — such as a publishing company, a tea plantation and valuable land in north Taipei on which the Foundation built its television station and humanities center. There have also been donations of factories, land, homes, offices and stocks. Its hospitals and schools are private and receive fees from those who use them. But most projects, including the building of new homes, schools and hospitals, its bone marrow bank, charity, overseas aid and television station, do not generate income and need substantial capital. Donors can choose how their money is spent — overseas aid, medical work, education, the television station, charity or a particular construction project. Of NT$100 given, fewer than NT$5 is spent on administrative costs. The paid professional staff is limited; the majority of the work is done by unpaid volunteers.

Over the past ten years, Tzu Chi's global footprint has greatly expanded, reaching Haiti and the Dominican Republic, Chile and Argentina, Jordan, Turkey, Pakistan, Nepal, Malaysia, Indonesia, Southern Africa and Poland, where it brings material and spiritual aid to Ukrainian refugees. One of its most remarkable foreign projects is the El Menahil ('Oasis' in Arabic) International School in the Sultangazi District of Istanbul. It teaches nearly five hundred students from Syrian refugee families with Syrian teachers who are also refugees; its diplomas are accredited by the Turkish government and other countries, including the United States. Its medium of instruction is Arabic, not Turkish, the language of Turkey. It has also classes in Turkish and adult literacy in Arabic for Syrians who were illiterate because they had received no education. For the first time in their lives, they can read the Quran. It is remarkable that a Buddhist charity from the other side of the world has been able to set up such a school for Muslim refugees from Syria. Establishing a school requires detailed government approval. An Islamic country, Turkey is suspicious of people coming to proselytize. Taiwan has no diplomatic relations with Turkey; raising funds for such an ambitious undertaking was no simple matter. El Menahil is a symbol of the success of Tzu Chi's international expansion. Another important initiative since 1990 has been recycling and environmentalism, which have become a core mission of the Foundation. It has more than 10,000 recycling centres in nineteen countries, where over 112,000 volunteers work; many are older than sixty-five.

For me, the most powerful memory of their work overseas was on a hillside over Durban in KwaZulu-Natal, South Africa. I was accompanying a group of Zulu ladies, members of the Foundation, who were visiting patients suffering from AIDS and their families. This was the area of the world worst affected by the disease. In the apartheid era, it had been a black township and was still where the poorest people lived. As we approached the house of a patient, the ladies broke out into beautiful hymns, loud enough so that those in the house could hear. After entering the house, they comforted the family and inquired whether the patient was taking the medicine and had sufficient quantities of it. In this cold and bleak house, they radiated love and warmth. They showed the same warmth to me. Then one said with a smile: "you are lucky to be with us. If you (a white) were here on your own, you would be robbed, and possibly worse." After embracing the family members, the ladies moved on to the next house. I reflected to myself: "a Buddhist charity in distant Taiwan can inspire such good in a Christian country on the other side of the world." Later I asked Gladys Ngema, one of the ladies, about her involvement in the movement. Staring me full in the eyes, she said: "when I die, I do not want to go to Paradise, but to Hualien." Overcome, I was lost for words.

Master Cheng Yen is the founder and leader of Tzu Chi. She is one of the "Great Mountains" of Buddhism in Taiwan and the only one alive now. Born in May 1937, she was 86 in 2023. Her charisma has been critical to the success of her movement. The same is true of the Masters of the other three major Buddhist movements. The founder of Fo Guang Shan (FGS) was Master Hsing Yun who passed away on February 5, 2023, aged ninety-five. About 30,000 people from five continents attended his funeral on February 13 at the FGS centre outside Kaohsiung, which he founded in 1967. The participants included President Tsai Ing-wen, the Prime Minister and other political leaders. Tsai gave a Presidential Citation Award and a letter for the late Master, praising him for establishing five universities and three hundred monasteries around the world. While Master Cheng Yen was born in Taiwan, Master Hsing Yun and the other two Masters were born in the Mainland and received their early education and training there. They came to Taiwan in 1949. The island has provided the conditions for them to establish global Buddhist movements — impossible if they had stayed in the Mainland.

FGS has an estimated ten million followers around the world, with two hundred branch temples in twenty countries, a university in Los Angeles and, in Taiwan, a daily newspaper, publishing house, radio station and television station. Master Hsing Yun wrote more than 100 books, which have been translated into twenty languages. In Taiwan, FGS runs orphanages, libraries, free mobile medical clinics, homes for the elderly and drug rehabilitation programs in prisons.

Unlike the other three Masters in Taiwan, Master Hsing Yun engaged with Mainland China. He first returned there in 1989, leading a delegation of monks to meet senior Buddhist officials. But, in 1990, he became persona non grata when he gave sanctuary in his Los Angeles temple to Xu Jiatun, director of the Xinhua News Agency in Hong Kong, who fled the country after the crackdown on student protests in June 1989; Beijing asked him not to. After rehabilitating him four years later, Beijing gave Master Hsing Yun one hundred thirty-three hectares of near Yixing to build the Temple of Great Awareness, complete with an art museum, meeting hall and giant statue of the Buddha. The local government offered to rename a nearby lake after him, but he refused. "The development of China cannot rely alone on material things and the economy," he said. "It is very important to purify the spirit, control the temperament, cure the heart, have a global outlook and raise the level of morality." He believed that building Buddhism meant involvement in politics. "In the history of China, Buddhism has suffered persecution several times, but each revival of Buddhism has come with the support of high-ranking officials," he said. He met three Chinese leaders, including Xi Jinping.

7
____

Too Much Freedom?

President Chiang Ching-kuo died on January 13, 1988, and was succeeded by Vice-President Lee Teng-hui. It was the end of the Chiang dynasty that had ruled the Republic of China since 1927. He had made it clear none of his three sons would succeed him. At the time, the foreign media was unsure how to assess Lee. He was the first native Taiwanese in its history to become head of state. Before Chiang appointed him Mayor of Taipei in 1978, he had made his career as an agricultural economist. He did not belong to the Mainland elite that had governed Taiwan since 1949. Some reports said Lee would be a transitional figure until the next presidential election in 1990, when he would hand over the position to a member of the Mainland elite. Certainly, members of that elite, including Song Mei-ling, widow of Chiang Kai-shek, did not trust Lee; they tried to prevent him becoming chairman of the ruling Kuomintang elite, the position essential to control the government. But they failed. In July 1988, Lee named a new Central Committee of the party; sixteen of the thirty-one members were Taiwanese, the first time in history that they had outnumbered the Mainlanders.

Lee's strengths were the facts that Chiang Ching-kuo had chosen him as his successor; a dense network of contacts among civil society through his experience as Mayor of Taipei and then Governor of Taiwan Province, and membership of the Presbyterian Church. He enjoyed popularity among Taiwan people who wanted one of their own as president and liked a leader fluent in Taiwanese. They also wanted a democratic system suitable to a country with Taiwan's high level of education and economic prosperity. Lee's weaknesses were limited ties with Tthe Mainland elite, especially the military, police and secret police, the Taiwan Garrison Command. They were the centers of Mainlander power; they had always opposed giving too much power to Taiwanese because, they argued, this would lead to calls for independence and a war with the Mainland.

Foreign skepticism about Lee turned out to be completely wrong. He proved to be a masterly politician, with a detailed agenda and the ability to implement it, despite strong opposition within his own party. His first job was to release political prisoners, many held for decades during the Chiang period. The most famous was Sun Li-jen, one of the most successful generals during the war with Japan. He earned the name 'Rommel of the East'. The Americans considered him the most capable general in the Chinese army. In 1950, Chiang Kai-shek named him Commander-in-Chief of the Chinese Army and commander of the Taiwan Defence Command. Probably because of his eminence and close ties with the Americans, Chiang suspected him. In August 1955, he was put under house arrest, on suspicion of planning a coup; more than three hundred of his subordinates were arrested. He remained under house arrest until Lee released him on March 20, 1988. His funeral in November 1990 was conducted with full military honors and attended by the Ministry of National Defense. Later a government investigation cleared his name. In January 2011, President Ma Ying-jeou formally apologized to his family.

Lee's next objective was to democratize the election system.

He offered generous pensions to the members of the National Assembly, which had since 1949 chosen the president. In March 1989, they were each offered NT$5.46 million to step down; some refused to accept it. In February 1990, the Assembly met to choose the president. Lee and his vice-presidential candidate faced a challenge from Lin Yang-gang, also a Taiwanese, and his candidate for vice-president, Chiang Wei-kuo, younger brother of Ching-kuo. Lee won the vote and secured another term as President.

Then, from March 16 to 22, university students began a sit-in at the Chiang Kai-shek Memorial Hall in downtown Taipei. They demanded an end to the National Assembly, retirement of Mainlanders who had occupied posts for decades and the political system to be fully democratic. The protests were peaceful and did not end in violence, like those in Beijing nine months earlier. Lee met student representatives and agreed to convene a National Affairs Conference to discuss their demands. Held from June 28 to July 4, 1990, it was open to a wide range of people and opinions, including a media now able to report freely. Lee used the conference to push the reforms he wanted. He implemented these in 1991 — the old members of the National Assembly retired, its size was reduced from 613 to 327 seats and that of the Legislative Yuan (Parliament) from 220 to 161. In the election in December 1991, the Kuomintang won 71 percent of the vote and 254 seats in the new NA, against 24 percent and 66 seats for the opposition Democratic Progressive Party (DPP). In elections for the Legislative Yuan in the autumn of 1992, the KMT won 53 percent of the vote and 102 seats, against 50 seats for the DPP. The campaign was heated and people voted in record numbers. Lee's first five years as president were a success. He had defeated opponents within his party, reformed the NA and held democratic elections for the Parliament.

On August 1, 1992, Lee disbanded the Taiwan Garrison Command. It was the main security instrument of martial law and the White Terror; it was believed to be responsible, directly or indirectly, for extrajudicial murders, arrests and detentions. This abolition was extremely popular with the Taiwan public.

On March 23, 1996, Taiwan held its first election for president chosen by popular mandate. It was a historic day—the first such election in Greater China. Lee won with 54 percent of the popular vote, while the DPP candidate won 21 percent and two KMT rebel candidates won 24.9 percent between them. Lee was helped by military exercises and live-fire drills carried out by thousands of PLA soldiers in the weeks leading up to the vote. These disgusted Taiwan people and persuaded them not to vote for candidates promising closer ties with China.

It was the evening of June 30, 1997, and I found myself at a Guangzhou Sports Stadium seething with people. They had gathered to take part in a government celebration of the return of Hong Kong to the motherland the next day. There were bands, marches and speeches by officials. The atmosphere was warm and buzzing. As far as I could see, I was the only Big-Nose present. A journalist walked over with his camera crew. "How about an interview?" he said. I thought about it and decided to decline. His editor wanted only one answer to his questions. I could not honestly give it. Opinion in Hong Kong about the return was sharply divided—some welcomed it, some opposed it and many were anxious about the future. This answer he could not broadcast. I explained this to the journalist and he graciously accepted it. He walked on, looking for others to interview.

A few days later, I returned to Hong Kong and was told by my editor to go to Taipei. The government there had invited journalists from different countries to hear its position on the 'one country, two systems' formula Beijing was implementing in Hong Kong and had offered to Taiwan. During the flight to Taipei, I was next to a black lady journalist from South Africa; she explained the complexities of her country after the end of apartheid five years earlier. 'Liberation' was never so simple. All of us on the plane felt we were covering one of the major stories in the world. Hong Kong had returned to China, Macau would follow two years later—what about Taiwan, the last remaining piece? At the airport, we were met by government officials and taken to our hotel.

We soon learned the answer to the question on Taiwan's future. We were summoned to an address by President Lee Teng-hui at the Taipei Guest House, a hundred meters from the Presidential Palace; it was an imposing building with high Roman pillars in the style of the French Second Empire. It was built by two prominent Japanese architects from 1899 to 1901; it was the residence of the Japanese Governor-General until he moved into the Palace in 1920. Crown Prince Hirohito stayed there when visiting Taiwan. After 1949, it became a state guest house, to receive visiting VIPs or for celebrations. It was an appropriate venue for an address of historic importance. The President started to speak. I had difficulty with his accent. Mandarin was his third language, after Taiwanese and Japanese. I whispered this to an official of the Foreign Ministry. "No problem," he said. "You are not the first to say this. We have written copies of the speech here." He gave me the text. His message was very clear. "Hong Kong will be governed under the 'one country, two systems' formula. We will not. We do not accept this formula," he said. He went on to talk about the history and development of Taiwan, but he had given us the headline. It was less than a week since July 1. It was an easy story to write—"Taiwan does not want 'one country, two systems.' " That evening, I made a telephone call to my editor in Hong Kong, a non-Chinese.

"Please could you take the next plane to Taipei?" I asked. "I am too low-ranking to have an interview with the President. But he would give one to you, as editor. This is the biggest story in the world at the moment."

He did not take long to reply, "No, I will not come." Agitated, I said this was a great news opportunity that would be good for the paper. But he was not open to discussion. Much better than I, he had understood how the political winds in Hong Kong had changed. Reporting the news from Taiwan was fine, but it would be unwise to give President Lee the prominence of a front-page interview with the editor. It was my first lesson about post-1997 Hong Kong.

Today, even after his death, Lee remains a very divisive figure in Taiwan. My 'green' friends revere him as the 'father of democracy'—he turned a one-party state into a multi-party democracy and gave the people the right to choose their president, their parliament and whether they want to be part of China. My 'blue' friends do not contest these achievements but say he was a 'traitor'. How could a man who believed in Taiwan's independence become the head of the KMT, the party founded in China that believes, finally, in a reunited country? They say that to secure and prolong his own power, he concealed his real beliefs.

My next visit to Taiwan was to cover the presidential election in March 2000. It was the second in which the public could choose their leader. It offered an unexpected opportunity to the opposition DPP to win for the first time. This was because two senior members of the Kuomintang, Lien Chan and James Soong, were both running as candidates. Lien was the KMT candidate. Angry at not being given the nomination himself, Soong was running as an independent; for this, the party expelled him. In previous elections, the KMT usually secured about sixty percent of the vote. This meant that, if Lien and Soong split this vote, the DPP candidate, Chen Shui-bian, could win, even without a plurality. Many countries require the winning candidate to have more than fifty percent of the votes—with a run-off, if necessary—but not Taiwan. This meant that, in terms of news, Chen and the DPP were the hot story.

It was an exciting assignment. No-one knew the outcome of the election. On the first night in my hotel, I turned on the television. It carried two advertisements from the DPP. The first was about Chen and called him 'the son of Taiwan'; it had footage of residents of the Guantian Township near Tainan in southwest Taiwan where he was born and grew up. Speaking in Taiwanese, a shoe repairman, a noodle seller and a shopkeeper recounted stories of the young Chen. The message was clear: he is a local Taiwanese boy from a humble background.

The second advertisement showed a government official being driven rapidly in a black limousine with an urgent message for Lien Chan, then Prime Minister. He gets out of the car next to a golf course; there a man in a black suit and white gloves puts his hand to his lips and whispers that the Premier is too busy with his golf game to receive the document. The message: Lian is privileged, arrogant and cut off from common people. Whether all this was true, I could not say. But the advertisements were cleverly made to deliver the message that Chan was a man of the people and Lien a member of the elite.

What was unquestionable were Chen's modest origins. He was the son of a rural laborer, the lowest rank in the social order. His father had no land of his own and had to rely on others to give him work; some days there was none. The young Chen was an outstanding student, first at the top high school in Tainan and later at National Taiwan University (NTU), where he graduated with a law degree. We needed a profile of him, I thought. So I went to his home village and asked the local DPP office to arrange an interview with his mother. Since she did not speak Mandarin, the office sent a DPP official to translate from Taiwanese into Mandarin. We sat on wooden chairs in the courtyard of the modest one-story brick house where she lived. It was indeed a dramatic story she had to tell.

"When he was born (in October 1950), he was such a weak baby that we thought he would not survive. I took him to the local temple and asked the nun there for help. She examined him and told me to add an additional character 水 (shui, water) to his name. So he became Chen Shui-bian, instead of Chen Bian. Thanks to the nun and the new character, his health improved. Our family was very poor, so he walked across the fields to school in his bare feet; we could not afford shoes. Fortunately, he was a gifted student and did well in his studies." Her son's rise was certainly a tribute to Taiwan's education system. In how many countries in the world, I wondered, could a child of a landless farmer became a potential president?

The election was bitter and intense; it aroused enormous public enthusiasm. As we walked the streets, all of us journalists felt it. It was the first time in Taiwan — in fact in Chinese history — that an election was being held whose outcome had not been pre-determined. Many narratives were being played out. One was the hope of DPP supporters that their candidate would win for the first time. Another was the fight between Lien and Soong for the KMT vote. Each believed that he should be the only candidate; if he were, he would win comfortably. Of the two, Soong was the better and more popular politician. The television advertisement had been correct to say that Lien came from a wealthy family of landlords and merchants. He was born in August 1936 in X'ian to a Taiwanese father and a Mainland Chinese mother. Like Chen, he graduated from NTU and earned a PhD in political science from the University of Chicago. He had an impressive career in public service — but a patrician manner more suitable for the Chiang-era than the new rough-and-tumble of democratic campaigning; you need to shake hands and share jokes with mothers holding their babies. In this heated atmosphere, everyone had something to say, an opinion to express. As they watched a debate on television, people in a restaurant could easily start shouting at one other. The newspapers, both pro-KMT and pro-DPP, were full of information and comment.

The shadow over the election was Mainland China. It obviously wanted Lien or Soong to win. But, for them, was this positive or negative? For a journalist, the campaign was a pleasure to cover. Everyone had an opinion and was eager to express it; sometimes you had to stop them talking. There was a wide variety of opinions, too, in the media — a far cry from the 'hall of a single voice of the martial law era. . Each evening my notebook was bulging with too much material; it needed severe editing to cut it to the required length for the story.

So it came to Election Day, March 18. In the morning I went to the elementary school in Taipei where Chen's wife, Wu Shu-chen, was voting. Her arrival was a poignant moment. An assistant pushed her in a wheelchair. This was the result of an accident on November 18, 1985. She and her husband were visiting DPP supporters in Tainan County when a farm vehicle burst through the crowd and ran over her three times; this left her paralyzed. Some DPP supporters said the driver of the vehicle, a farm laborer, had been paid by the KMT to assassinate Chen — this was still the martial law period. Whatever the cause, she suffered this terrible injury for the sake of her husband's political career. Well-educated, she could have had a good career in law or business. I wondered how she felt in heart toward her husband. She voted in one of the classrooms of the school. I asked her what it would be like to be First Lady. She did not reply but looked at me from her wheelchair with a sad expression. That is the image I retain of her. As the hours passed, the excitement mounted. The turnout was 83 percent, an extraordinarily high level; it reflected the enthusiasm of the Taiwan public for their hard-won democracy. Fortunately, the count was done that same day. In the evening, we learned the result—Chen won 39.3 percent of the vote, Soong 36.84 percent Lien 23.1 percent. Taiwan would have its first DPP president, and the first peaceful transfer of power in Chinese history from a ruling to an opposition party.

Emotions on the street were running high. KMT supporters stood with their head in their hands. "We won sixty percent of the votes but lost. How fair is that?" one man asked. I found a man in his forties weeping. "I am an engineer. For the first time in our history, we have one of our own as president," he said. "Yes, Lee Teng-hui is a Taiwanese but represented the Kuomintang. The DPP is our party. I cannot find the words to express my emotions." In terms of news, this was the most dramatic outcome—a milestone in the 5,000-year history of China.

In the next election on March 20, 2004, Chen was reelected president by the narrowest of margins—he won 50.11 percent of the votes, against 49.89 percent for his Kuomintang opponent, Lien Chan, with James Soong as vice-presidential candidate. It was a difference of less than 30,000 votes out of the 12.9 million cast. Considering that, four years earlier, Lien and Soong had between them attracted nearly 60 percent of the votes, this was a considerable achievement by Chen; it showed his ability to broaden the electoral base of the DPP. Turnout was again very high, at 80.28 percent. With absentee ballots not allowed, about 20,000 Taiwanese returned home from North America and more than 100,000 came from Mainland China to vote. On March 19, the day before the voting, Chen and Vice-Presidential running mate Annette Lu were riding in an open convertible Jeep in Tainan when they were both shot. Chen received a flesh wound eight centimeters long and two centimeters deep. Another bullet grazed Lu's knee. Both left hospital later that day without needing surgery. Since such violence had been unknown in Taiwan, it provoked great shock. Police quickly announced that the crime was not politically motivated and that Mainland China was not involved. KMT friends, angry at the defeat of their candidate, suggested Chen had staged the assassination attempt to gain more votes. I did not know what to believe—sympathy votes after such an attack, yes, but how to stage it without injuring your candidates?

One morning in 2007, I was reading the *United Daily News*, where I worked in the early 1980s. It remains today one of Taiwan's most important newspapers. The headline read: 'Stolen Treasures'. The story had a floor map of Sogo, an upmarket department store in downtown Taipei. The map showed the desks where Wu Shu-chen had purchased diamond rings, jewelry and other luxury items. I had two emotions. One was that this was a good piece of journalism, informing the public what the wife of the president had bought and where. The other was a sense of tragedy—that a talented woman trapped in a wheelchair had stolen public money to satisfy her own desires.

On August 15, 2008, three months after the end of his second term, Chen and Wu announced their resignation from the DPP. "I let everyone down, caused you humiliation and failed to meet your expectations," Chen said. "I express my deepest regrets to all DPP members and supporters." The items from Sogo were the tip of the iceberg. Later in August investigators announced Chen had $21 million in overseas banks held in the name of family members. In November 2010, the Taiwan High Court ruled that Chen and Wu would have to serve seventeen and a half years in prison for corruption and bribery. Given Wu's state of health, this was difficult for the Taichung prison where she was sent. In February 2011, the prison hospital ruled that she was too ill to serve; she was released from jail and put under house arrest. For most Taiwan people, this is the memory they have of Chen — corruption and prison. He was the first Chinese president in history to be convicted by a court of a crime and sentenced to prison. This shame overshadowed his achievements in attaining high office and running the country for eight years. The scandal handed the 2008 presidential election to the candidate of the Kuomintang, Ma Ying-jeou.

In visits to Taiwan during the Chen era between 2000 and 2008, I often felt this democratic fervor. People were eager to express their views on political parties and their leaders, Mainland China, whether Taiwan should have nuclear power plants and many other subjects. You felt as if they were making up for the lost years of silence under martial law. Sometimes, I thought, this democratic transformation had been too successful. Perhaps such diverse and lively opinions make a country difficult to govern — it is hard to reach a consensus on policy and stick with it. Many older people expressed this view. During the Chiang era, they said, political debate was limited; the government could draw up long-term economic policies and implement them. Now there is too much debate and policies keep changing, so much is short term.

But I did not hear political chatter from members of the Tzu Chi Foundation. Master Cheng Yen tells her disciples not to take part in political demonstrations; time is too precious, and it should be used to help those who are suffering. Her disciples were well educated and well informed. I am sure they had their own opinions on the issues of the day. But, when I was discussing matters to do with the Foundation, we did not talk politics. I think her reason had to do with harmony. To make her organization work smoothly, people must have a broad level of agreement and implement the tasks in hand. Arguing over politics consumes time and energy; it creates conflict between people. Once a volunteer told me that it was natural for people to have different opinions on what projects to take up and how to implement them. "But we deal with this in a soft, well-mannered way," he said.

I was reminded of these two cultures one weekend in 2007; it was a seminar at the Foundation headquarters in Hualien. It consisted of meetings, lectures and Buddhist ceremonies. We slept in a dormitory on a wooden floor in a large building. As a person who likes to get up early, I thought I could handle this comfortably. On Saturday, I woke up at 4:45 a.m., early enough, I thought. Not so—I looked around to see nearly all men in the room had already got up, folded their sleeping bags neatly, had a wash and gone to attend the first event. Then I remembered that all of them had served at least two years in the military, had slept in worse places than this, and got up even earlier. By Sunday morning, I was flagging badly, unable to keep pace with my fellow participants. So I made an excuse; they graciously forgave the Big-Nose, and I left the seminar after lunch. Back in the lobby of the hotel in the city, the television was broadcasting President Chen at a news conference. He was rambling, speaking partly in Mandarin and partly in Taiwanese. A member of staff told me that he was talking about the allegations of corruption against him and his family. He did not look like a president. Hotel guests in the lobby were venting their anger loudly at the television. We were back in the political bull-pit.

In 2019, Joint Publishing of Hong Kong graciously accepted my proposal for a book on Faina, the Russian wife of Chiang Ching-kuo. We called it *China's Russian Princess*. There were many excellent biographies, in Chinese and English, of Chiang Ching-kuo, but none in English and only a handful in Chinese about Faina Ipat'evna Vakhreva, her full name. From living in Taipei in 1981 to 1983, I remember she was a secretive person. She never appeared in public; most people knew nothing about her, except that she was Russian.

Her story turned out to be even more extraordinary that I had imagined — in the winter of 1933, she met an ebullient young Chinese on the assembly line of a heavy machinery factory in Yekaterinburg, the city in the center of Russia where the Bolsheviks murdered Tsar Nicholas II and his family in July 1918. The young Ching-kuo was charming and humorous; he spoke and wrote Russian fluently and could dance and drink almost as well as his colleagues. From there, it was a long and tortuous journey for Faina to Shanghai and Chongqing through two wars. Then to Taipei where she lived from April 1949 until her death there on December 15, 2004. If you want to know her story, please read the book; there are editions in English and Chinese.

What I would like to describe here is the writing of the book and what it told us about Taiwan. One reason for choosing people and subjects in Taiwan is that it is open and accessible. Like most people, I can go there without a visa. There are excellent bookshops and libraries and university and research centers where people are willing to speak to you. When you start work on a book, you do not know what you will find. But you know that in Taiwan there is material waiting for you to find. The Academica Historica (國史館) was a good example. This is the institution, just behind the Presidential Palace in central Taipei, which stores documents of the history of the Republic of China, including its presidents. I went in search of images of Faina and her family. Aware of the likely security, I took my passport and other documents to prove my bona fides, to show to the soldiers or police on duty. To my surprise, there were none—only two polite middle-aged women at the front desk asking how they could help. They directed me to a room down a corridor that was full of files and computers. There I told two more charming ladies what I needed. They showed me to a computer and provided dozens of images; I chose about thirty-five and paid a modest fee for the right to use them. They were a great asset to the book since few people, even in Taiwan, had seen them.

Another find was the Astoria Café and Bakery on Wuchang Street, near Taipei's main railway station. This was opened as a Russian restaurant in October 1949 by six White Russians, who had, like the Kuomintang, fled the Mainland. During the 1950s, it was a favorite place for Faina and her husband for Russian food, Russian wine and to sing and dance on the tables. I was graciously received by the manager who explained the history of the Astoria. She was a classmate of Faina's granddaughter and went to visit her at the family home; she had met Faina often. The most important interview was with Elizabeth Chiang, widow of one of Faina's three sons. She spoke at length and very movingly about her mother-in-law.

But that was the best I could do with members of the Chiang family and those who worked and lived with them. James Soong and Ma Ying-jeou both served as secretaries of Chiang Ching-kuo and saw Faina often; they declined a meeting. So did John Chiang Hsiao-yen, son of Ching-kuo and a mistress in mainland China. He had a distinguished career in the Foreign Service and then in senior positions in the government and the Kuomintang. I also failed to arrange a meeting with one of Ching-kuo's doctors, elderly but still active in medicine. All were gracious enough to reply by e-mail, either in person or through their staff. I asked Taiwan friends to explain this low strike rate. One answered, "First, your relations (關系, guanxi) with the Kuomintang are too thin. You need a friend to call these people and ask them to receive you. You do not have enough connections with the party. Secondly, everything in Taiwan is politicized. We have 24-hour news channels looking for things to report. While Faina was not involved in politics at all, things said about her could be used." So it was the excellent bookshops of Taipei that saved me. There I found two biographies of Faina, an autobiography by one of Chiang Ching-kuo's bodyguards and one by the Baptist chaplain of the Chiang family. They contained rich and detailed material about Faina and her life.

On February 28, 2023, Taipei Mayor Chiang Wan-an went to New Park in downtown Taipei to remember the victims of the government crackdown that began that day in 1947 and set off the White Terror. He was accompanied by former President Ma Ying-jeou. Chiang is the son of John Chiang Hsiao-yen and great-grandson of former President Chiang Kai-shek, the man who ordered the crackdown. But a visit of forgiveness and memorial could not pass in quiet solemnity. The city mobilized one hundred eighty police to protect the mayor and his party against protesters. They screamed, "Murderer and assassin, kneel and apologize," in reference to his great-grandfather, and held up banners with this message. A week earlier, fifty civilian groups had issued a statement saying that Chiang should not visit the memorial; his presence there was a "humiliation for the people of Taiwan". After seventy-six years, the wounds of February 28, 1947, had still not healed.

When I lived in Taipei in the 1980s, I was walking down a narrow street with a friend. We passed the compound of a house with high walls, a closed door and an armed soldier standing guard. After we had walked beyond the hearing of the soldier, my friend whispered, "That is the home of General Peng Meng-chi, one of commanders during the 1947 crackdown. His house needs an armed guard around the clock. He could be assassinated." In those days, it was not allowed to speak in public about those tragic events.

After he became president, Lee Teng-hui lifted the taboo on the White Terror. On February 28, 1995, a monument to the victims of the killings was unveiled in New Park. Lee issued a formal apology to a hundred family members of the victims, who were carrying yellow roses. It was a first step toward reconciliation. Two years later, a museum describing the events opened in a former radio station next to the park. Lee also set up a commission to establish the facts of what happened and pay compensation to families of the victims. It estimated the number of those killed at 18,000 to 28,000.

In 2003, the next President, Chen Shui-bian, presented rehabilitation certificates to the victims of the incident and their families. An official report in 2006 said Chiang Kai-shek was primarily responsible for the crackdown. A total of 20,340 relatives of the victims received compensation, as much as NT$6 million for the loss of their loved ones. In February 2017, President Tsai Ing-wen told a visiting group of family members of victims Taiwan had lost almost a whole generation of its elite due to the mistakes committed by the authoritarian rulers of that time. "Even today, Taiwanese are still suffering from the consequences of the 2-28 Incident," she said. She praised Germany for facing up to its historical mistakes. "The German government, academics and the private sector have continued to probe the historical facts in a bid to more carefully dig out the truth and have continued to prosecute Nazi war criminals," she said.

Taiwan has done more than many lands in facing its past and atoning for its mistakes. Former President Ma has made more than thirty visits to the Memorial in the park. But some issues remain hard to resolve—was martial law itself illegal? Should the individuals responsible for enforcing the White Terror be prosecuted? Should all the official archives be open? Friends on the Kuomintang side told me thatin the first three decades after 1949, Taiwan faced a real threat of invasion by the Mainland. This meant the KMT needed special measures to deter the threat. It was not like governing Holland or Ireland, countries with no external enemy. In his remarks that day, Mayor Chiang Wan-an apologized for the police confiscation of contraband cigarettes from the woman in Taipei on February 27, 1947. That was what set off the nationwide protests. "I respect every kind of opinion," he said. "Taiwan is a democratic and diverse society. The Taipei city government will continue its effort to confront the history and restore the truth." Mayor Chiang believed it his duty to visit the memorial on that day, I think; but it could not be a normal visit.

In 2011, the Republic of China celebrated its 100th birthday. It was an important year. As a start, the government invited 100 couples to the Presidential Palace in the early morning of January 1 for a mass wedding overseen by President Ma Ying-jeou. "This is a milestone in history, our country is one hundred years old," he told them.

The government invited thousands of foreign guests to attend the celebrations, including me. One day, other foreign journalists and I were invited into the Palace to meet Ma, Vice-President Vincent Siew and their wives. We queued up. When my turn arrived, I shook the President's hand and bowed. From Hunan Province, he is shorter than I, so it made a good photograph. Everyone in the palace was in a joyful mood. An official of the Foreign Ministry told me, "We are one hundred years old today. We have passed the average age of a Chinese dynasty. We are good to go for the second century." On the walls hung images of Dr Sun Yat-sen, father of the republic and the first president who held office from January to March 1912. He died just thirteen years later, in March 1925. During his lifetime, China was wracked by conflicts between warlords and did not achieve the stable government he had dreamed of. He could never have imagined his republic celebrating its 100th birthday in Taipei, so far from the Mainland cities where he lived.

The largest foreign delegation for the 100th birthday came from Japan. Sixty-six members of the Japanese Diet came to join the celebrations, the largest group of Japanese politicians ever to visit Taiwan. It was in part to show the gratitude of the Japanese people to the government and citizens of Taiwan for their donations to the victims of the terrible earthquake and tsunami in March that year. As we explained in Chapter Three, donations from Taiwan were more than from any other land and the size of the group also showed the close relations between the two sides. In 2011, bilateral trade was a record $70.4 billion; the number of Japanese visitors to the island reached 1.29 million, surpassing for the first time the number of Taiwanese going the other way. President Ma said bilateral relations were their best ever.

With other foreign guests, I stayed at government expense in the five-star Ambassador Hotel in downtown Taipei. At breakfast one morning, I was sitting next to an elderly Japanese man with silver hair; we were admiring the trees in a park next to the hotel turning brown. "I love coming to Taiwan," he said. "People are polite and many speak Japanese. In some places, I think I am at home. Recently, however, many Mainland tourists have been coming to Taiwan. I am not so comfortable with them. Many are anti-Japanese. For me, better is fewer Mainlanders."

One morning I walked into the entrance lobby. Officials of the Foreign Ministry were busy greeting the VIPs. "This is quite a headache," one said. "How do we get all the names right?" Many of the visitors came from small countries in Africa that had diplomatic relations with Taiwan. She said, "I struggle with the names of the countries, not to speak of the names of the dignitaries themselves."

What struck me was how Taiwan people, especially the young, were growing away from China. A survey by National Chengchi University in 1992 found twenty-six percent of Taiwan people identifying themselves as Chinese; by 2010, the figure had fallen to four percent. The DPP government between 2000 and 2008 had promoted the use of the Taiwanese and Hakka languages and the culture of the Aboriginals who had lived in the island before the Han Chinese came. Aboriginal dancing was included in the anniversary events. President Ma spoke in Taiwanese. Young people cherished their civil liberties, freedom of speech and democracy and a diversity of newspapers, magazines, books and films impossible in the Mainland. "All this has created a common Taiwan identity," said Eric Li, a friend and journalist. "Marriage between Taiwanese and Mainlanders has become more common. Young people like Japanese and American culture, as well as books and films created here. Also there is a common anger at being excluded from international organizations because of China. People consider this so unfair."

The main event on October 10 was the military parade through the city center and in front of the Palace always held on that day. In his speech, President Ma said that as China moved toward becoming a more prosperous society, its people would also want more democracy and greater rule of law. "Such a desire has never been a monopoly of the West, but is the right of all humankind. We firmly support the pursuit of the people of Hong Kong to directly and democratically elect their own leader," he said. He said that, just as Deng Xiaoping had allowed some in China to become rich first, so Beijing could allow Hong Kong to go democratic first.Seen from 2023, it seems so far away. Thirteen months after Ma's speech, Xi Jinping became General Secretary of China's Communist Party. He is a committed Marxist-Leninist for whom party control of politics and the economy is paramount. After street protests in Hong Kong turned violent in 2019, Beijing passed the National Security Law for Hong Kong in June 2020. The democratic progress in Hong Kong went into reverse. Pro-democracy legislators and activists fled the city or were arrested or imprisoned. Major pro-democracy organizations, trade unions and media closed. In elections for the Legislative Council in December 2021, voter turnout was thirty percent, the lowest for any LegCo election in history. Hong Kong is the only city in the Mainland allowing such votes. Indeed, the gap between Taiwan and China seems to be growing wider and wider.

8

NATIONAL PALACE MUSEUM — TREASURES OF THE EMPEROR

In 2015, I was sitting in the reception room of the National Palace Museum (NPM) in Shilin, a northern district of Taipei. It was full of beautiful pieces of Chinese art. In walked Chou Kung-shin, the director, as smart and elegant as the pieces around her. I was preparing an article for Macao Magazine on the history of the museum and the pieces in it. The next hour and a half were hypnotic. Director Chou described the sixteen-year-long odyssey of the pieces from the Palace Museum in Beijing across China and to Taiwan. They crossed rivers and mountains and were hidden in basements, caves and temples. They survived the war with Japan and then the civil war, before arriving finally in Taiwan in 1948 and 1949. "No pieces were lost or stolen," she said. "This was due to the dedication of the staff and the protection of God. It was a miracle. The staff stayed with the pieces every day. They did not leave the pieces unattended. If the pieces were stored in a school, they slept in a school." They were like religious objects for the faithful.

I returned to Hong Kong and wrote the article for the magazine. But the space was too short to tell the story. I contacted Anne Lee, my beloved editor at Joint Publishing, and asked if she would accept a book on the subject. She graciously agreed, with versions in English and Chinese. So I headed back to Taipei to gather material. First stop was the library of the NPM. The head librarian, a lady as elegantly dressed as the director, walked toward me with a sheaf of materials under her arm. I had not said a word, but she knew everything already. "I think this is what you are looking for," she said. She was right—the sheaf contained the museum's official history and books by and about those staff who had cared for the pieces with dedication over so many years. All these greatly facilitated the task of writing the book—eye-witness accounts of the odyssey.

It was in April 1982 that I had first learned of the NPM. I went to interview an elderly gentleman named Han Lih-wu, seventy-nine, head of the Taipei branch of the World Anti-Communist League, in a modest office downtown. We talked of his work at the League and its role in the global movement; in 1990, it would change its name to World League for Freedom and Democracy. As I was leaving, Mr Han handed me an essay on the NPM. I discovered that, before the League, he had lived many lives— and the NPM was one of them. He held degrees from universities in Nanjing, London and Madison, Wisconsin. In the late 1920s, he returned to China to teach at Nanjing University. From 1931 to 1946, he headed the British-Chinese Educational Association. In 1944, he became Deputy Minister of Education. In the autumn of 1948, he was one of eight people called late at night to the Nanjing home of the Premier, who was also chairman of the NPM. Nanjing was the Nationalist capital. The agenda: to decide whether or not to move the art treasures to Taiwan "Not everyone agreed," said Han, who was secretary to the board of the museum. "Peace talks were going on between the communists and the Kuomintang. The Premier, also chairman of the board of the museum, kept telling us to wait. Finally, he said, 'If you insist on going, all right, but do it secretly.' "

The eight made a momentous decision. Since the People's Liberation Army was winning the civil war, they decided to ship the most valuable artifacts to Taiwan. On December 21, 1948, a naval vessel left Nanjing with 512 containers with items from the NPM, as well as important documents from the Academia Sinica, the National Central Library and the Ministry of Foreign Affairs. On January 6 and 30, 1949, two vessels carried more precious cargo, including 2,672 containers of pieces from the NPM. What arrived in Taiwan was one fifth of the total that had left Beijing in 1933. These became the pieces that visitors to the museum see today. When I got home, I put the essay from Mr Han in a box and forgot about it — until that meeting with Director Chou.

During the years I lived in Beijing, I saw the enormous importance of the Palace Museum. The center point of the city, it was the equivalent of the great cathedrals that dominate the main squares of European cities; they are both works of monumental architecture and also guardians of the nation's culture and history. The museum opened its doors on October 10, 1925. For five centuries before that, it had been the palace of the emperors; they had collected thousands of pieces of the finest porcelain, jades and bronzes and the imperial library, which included copies of every book printed under the emperors since 868 AD. The last dynasty, the Qing, fell in October 1911; this led to the establishment of the Republic of China. The new government allowed the last Emperor Pu Yi, then six years old, to go on living in the palace with his retinue of two thousand eunuchs, court ladies and retainers; it even gave him an allowance. How much more humanitarian than the French and Soviet revolutionaries in treating their emperors.

But Pu Yi found the generous allowance insufficient for his five-star lifestyle. He and his courtiers smuggled pieces out of the Palace and sold them in art shops in the city. To stop this, in November 1924, the government ordered him and all his courtiers to leave the Palace with two hours' notice; staff searched them thoroughly on their way out to see if they were hiding items inside their clothing. The government opened it as a museum on National Day, October 10, 1925. One member of the staff told to make an inventory ahead of the opening was an eighteen-year-old named Na Chih-liang, who had joined the museum that year. His autobiography was among the books the NPM librarian gave me. He was one of those devoted officials who accompanied the pieces in their odyssey across China and then came with them to Taiwan. He worked for the Museum from 1924 until 1975 — fifty-one years. "If its culture is lost, there is no hope of rebuilding the country," he said. He became one of the world's leading experts in jades.

In the late 1980s, I used to visit the Palace Museum in Beijing. It was a more profound experience than going to a normal museum — it had been an imperial palace for five centuries. Constructed from 1406 to 1420, it has 980 buildings covering more 720,000 square meters and more than 1.8 million pieces of art; only two percent were on display at any one time. It was the largest collection of wooden structures in the world. It had survived the many wars and upheavals of China through the centuries. During World War Two, the Japanese did not bomb it. In January 1949, one reason the KMT commander of the Beijing army surrendered to the surrounding PLA forces was to save the Imperial Palace. II, the .

So, as I walked through its rooms and imposing halls, I thought of the many episodes of Chinese history that had taken place there. I marveled at the elegant designs and red and yellow colors. Inside, I forgot about the communists, the Kuomintang and China of the 20th Century. Here was a place that stood above these political conflicts; it belonged to all Chinese. During those years, most Beijing people did not have the leisure nor the money to visit the palace. Especially, if you went on a weekday, you could have rooms entirely to yourself—as it was in imperial times, when entry was forbidden to ordinary people. The closest we have in Europe is the Palace of Versailles, but the Kings of France only lived there for limited periods, not the five consecutive centuries of the Ming and Qing dynasties. There is nowhere in the world that can compare to the Palace Museum.

In 1986, we heard a rumor that Italian film director Bernardo Bertolucci wanted to make a film about Pu Yi. Unlikely, we thought. The government had always refused permission to Chinese filmmakers to shoot within the Palace; with all its structures made of wood, the risk of a fire was too great. Why give permission to a non-Chinese, especially from Western Europe? We were wrong. Through charm and eloquence—or other means—Bertolucci persuaded the government to give him complete freedom within the Palace. The Chinese directors were not happy. *The Last Emperor* cost $23.8 million to make and needed 19,000 extras, including members of the PLA. It was a triumph. It won many awards and grossed $79 million at the box office around the world. As an advertisement for Beijing, it was a masterstroke. For the first time, people from Japan to Genoa and Penang to Pittsburgh saw the beauty and majesty of the Palace; the film helped to turn it into one of the world's most popular tourist destinations.

Now back to Taiwan. After the pieces arrived in 1948 and 1949, they were stored in warehouses of the Taichung Sugar Factory in central Taiwan. In April 1950, they were moved to a storehouse designed for them in Beigou, Wufeng, also in central Taiwan. They were safe there; but the location was too remote for any but a handful of visitors, Chinese or foreign. In 1961, many pieces were taken to the United States and shown in an exhibition for more than a year; thousands of people marveled at them. It was a huge success. Seeing the popularity of the pieces, the government decided they needed a home more accessible to the public. Another factor, I think, was a realization by President Chiang Kai-shek that he would not soon return to the mainland. The art pieces were the most popular items that visitors to Taiwan, Chinese and foreign, would want to see.

The government—more likely, President Chiang himself—chose a site in Shilin, in northern Taipei. It was not far from where the President lived. It had many advantages—the area was not densely populated and easy to protect; it was in front of a mountain in which the majority of pieces would be stored, while a small portion was put on display, to be rotated every three months. In 1960s Taiwan, security was always a priority. If there was an air attack, the pieces would be safe inside the mountain. The government held a competition for design of the building. The winner was Wang Da-hong, who had studied architecture at Cambridge and Harvard Universities; he was a leader in modernist architecture in Taiwan. He would later design the Sun Yat-sen Memorial Hall and Ministry of Foreign Affairs, two landmarks in Taipei. The government asked Wang to modify his design, but he refused. President Chiang liked traditional Chinese palace style. So the government chose instead a design by Huang Bao-yu in that style. Construction work began in March 1964 and was completed in August 1965.

The soft opening was held on November 12, 1965, the birthday of Dr Sun Yat-sen, ninety-nine years before. It opened to the public the next day, with 1,573 items including calligraphy, famous paintings, bronzes, tapestries, porcelains, jades, curios, rare books, and historical documents exhibited in fourteen galleries. The rest of the more than 600,000 pieces were stored in warehouses dug into of the mountain; access to them is strictly controlled. Going around the NPM is an experience quite different from visiting its elder brother in Beijing. The NPM is a modern, purpose-built museum, with excellent space, lighting and air control, to show the items at their best. Its elder brother in Beijing had been built as a palace for the emperor and his family; its curators have had to create a museum on this basis, without much of the sophisticated equipment found in a modern museum — no easy matter.

The money spent on the NPM was one of the best investments by the Kuomintang government in Taiwan. It has become the most popular tourist attraction in the island, for both Chinese and non-Chinese. The two record years were 5.4 million visitors in 2014 and 5.29 million in 2015. For people from the Mainland, it is a compulsory stop. In fact, they liked it so much that Taiwan people began, quietly, to complain there was no space for them. Friends told me that, if they planned a visit, they would find out when the Mainland tour groups were visiting and choose another time. Staff carried notices saying 'Quiet', to encourage their Mainlander cousins to keep their voices and mobiles down in deference to the solemnity of the pieces.

From the point of view of research, too, it has been a great success. It provides an excellent venue for scholars, domestic and foreign, to research the treasures of the museum. It publishes material in written form and on the internet. It earns revenue from selling tickets and books, postcards, paintings and other items in a large store next to the main entrance. It also earns money from licence agreements with fashion brands, restaurants and technology companies. They make clothing lines, merchandise and instant messaging stickers inspired by the treasures of the museum.

In the unfinished 'civil war' with the Mainland, construction of the NPM has a deeper meaning. It has provided a modern, state-of-the-art venue to display these treasures of Chinese history and safe, sophisticated storage facilities for the pieces not on display. It was part of the government's narrative to be the lawful government of China. During Mao's rule from 1949 until his death in 1976, the value of the NPM was beyond dispute. The Nationalist government said that it had brought the pieces to Taiwan to 'save' them from communist rule. During the Cultural Revolution from 1966 to 1976, Red Guards destroyed a great quantity of Chinese culture, including temples, monasteries, art works, antiques and other items. Mao ordered destruction of the 'Four Olds' — old culture, old customs, old habits and old ideas. The Red Guards did that or stole items for themselves or to sell to art shops. On August 18, 1966, Premier Zhou Enlai learned some Red Guards planned to destroy the Imperial Palace. He ordered the museum to be closed and the Beijing Garrison Command to take up defensive positions around its perimeter. The next day Red Guards put slogans on the outer walls, such as, "Burn the Forbidden City to the Ground" and "Smash the Palace." The Palace Museum was closed for ten years — unimaginable! During that decade, the NPM was every year receiving thousands of visitors, Chinese and foreign, to admire the treasures. The government's decision to bring them to Taiwan had been completely vindicated. As the years passed, the NPM developed a life of its own. It became beloved by Taiwan people as part of their heritage and identity and a source of national pride.

With the reform and open-door policy, China became a more 'normal' country. The guardians of the Palace Museum were able to give the same devotion to their pieces as their cousins in Taipei. More funding from the government enabled them to modernize and improve the museum and turn it into one of the world's most popular attractions. In 2019, the last year before

Covid, it attracted 19.3 million visitors. On December 31, 2022, it began work on a new branch in the Haidian district, with an investment of 2.1 billion yuan ($300 million) and a construction area of more than 100,000 square meters. It will display many pieces for which there is no space in the existing museum; it is also a place forrestoration, preservation and research of cultural treasures.

But politics has always been a shadow over the NPM. Since its foundation, it has never held exhibitions of its treasures on the Mainland; it fears it might not able to bring them back to Taiwan. Instead, it goes to countries that provide legal guarantees against seizure—Japan, South Korea, Germany, Austria, France, Australia and the United States. These are major exhibitions that attract thousands of visitors. The exhibitions have assumed a greater importance with Taiwan's increasing diplomatic isolation and exclusion from international organizations. They remind visitors of Taiwan's place in the world and that it is home to such an important museum. Without hard power, you use soft power.

Politics also dictate the NPM's relations with museums in the Mainland. During the eight-year presidency of Ma Ying-jeou from 2008 to 2016, relations between Taipei and Beijing improved. Director Chou used this opportunity to make a landmark visit to the Mainland in 2009. "Such visits are necessary if a museum wants to increase its substance and raise its profile," she said. "Exchanges of personnel for research, management, operation and marketing purposes are also important," she said. She signed an agreement with the PM to lend 37 Qing Dynasty treasures for the first joint exhibition in Taipei in October 2009. Another landmark was the reunion of two separated parts of a famous painting, *Dwelling in the Fuchu Mountain,* from the 14th Century. Its display in Taipei in 2011 was the first time it had been shown in its entirety for nearly four hundred years.

But in 2016, Tsai Ing-wen, candidate of the DPP, won the presidency and Beijing suspended official exchanges. The museums and those who work in them are hostages to these politics. Since 2022, a new issue has arisen. What would happen to the treasures in the event of a war between China and Taiwan? Is there a plan to evacuate the museum of the pieces to Japan or the US? The museum has strongly denied such suggestions. Chou says the safest place for the treasures was exactly where they are. "There are warehouses built in mountain tunnels to keep the treasures, and those warehouses are the safest places to store the artifacts. In the event of a military attack, the mountain would provide better protection. Normally an enemy force would not deliberately bombard important museums housing ancient artifacts, deemed to be the cultural treasures of all people in the world," she said.

By now, the reader will have gathered that it was a great good fortune to write a book on the two museums. The NPM provided much material and made their staff available for interviews. They were always helpful and courteous. I also made a trip to the Palace Museum in Beijing. I was too small a potato to meet the director. But he had given several interviews to the Chinese media; from these, I learned his philosophy and how he managed his museum. I met staff members who were helpful in answering questions and providing material. So the story was not difficult to write. What was difficult was facing questions from intellectuals in Beijing and Taipei asking for details of the jade and bronzes of particular dynasties. I tried to bluff, but my ignorance soon became apparent. Thousands of years of Chinese art are like a mighty ocean; I was like a paddle boat heaving up and down on the waves.

9

From US Handouts to King of Semi-Conductors

In 1981, I spent my first week in Taiwan in Hsinchu, in northwest Taiwan, with my friend, Wang Li. He graciously showed me around his city. We walked around; it was bustling, full of motorcycles and pick-up trucks carrying goods to and fro. We visited mom and pop shops and department stores, where we saw fans, garments, televisions and microwave ovens, all made in Taiwan. I was impressed, but Mr Wang was not. "Yes, we can export these goods to Japan, the United States and Europe, but how much do our firms really earn from them?" he said. "They are low-tech. What we need are high-tech products with a good profit margin. How else will we survive, an overcrowded island with a large defence budget?"

Forty years on, where are we? In 2022, Taiwan's GDP was $1.612 trillion and by purchasing power parity (PPP), ranked eighth in Asia and twenty-second in the world. In GDP per capita (PPP), it ranked fourteenth in the world. In one sector in particular, it has out-performed the world — semi-conductors. It produces ninety percent of the globe's advanced semi-conductors, astonishing for a small island with a population of only 23 million. Its most important company is Taiwan Semiconductor Manufacturing Company (TSMC). Its headquarters is in the Hsinchu Science

Park, established on December 15, 1980, not far from where Mr Wang and I were doing our window shopping. The Park is next door to the National Tsing Hua University, where Mr Wang was studying. Its semi-conductors are used in automobiles, mobile phones, jet fighters, computers and many other products.

It may not be an exaggeration to say the real estate in the Park occupied by TSMC and United Microelectronics Corporation, number two in the world in semi-conductors, is the most valuable in the world. If production at their two sites in Hsinchu stopped, industries all around the world would have to shut down—some say that it would be the end of globalization! Taiwan's economic ranking is a remarkable achievement for a land that has lived with the same military threat during those four decades, requiring a large defense budget. I remember what Mr Wang said during our tour, "Taiwan, Japan and South Korea are in the same boat. We have almost no natural resources outside agriculture; we rely on importing materials and exporting finished goods. All we have is the skill and hard work of our people."

Kuomintang rule in Taiwan did not begin auspiciously. The rebellion in 1947 and its ruthless suppression created a deep division between Taiwanese and Mainlanders. In 1946, the population was 6.1 million. Between that year and 1952, it increased by two million Mainlanders, with one million coming in 1949 and 1950. The majority were soldiers, civil servants and ordinary people who feared for their lives and livelihoods under communist rule. Most brought only what they could carry in a suitcase—plus gold, jewelry and other valuables hidden in their bras and underwear, as they told me. The government had to house, clothe and feed this flood of migrants and find them work. On the plus side, they included many of China's business and intellectual elite; they brought knowledge, experience and capital that would be vital to build the new state. One of the government's earliest policies, starting in April 1949, was land reform — first reducing rents and then transferring land to those who farmed it. For compensation, the landlords were given shares in four large state companies; many became entrepreneurs. Many historians believe if the Kuomintang had done the same thing in the Mainland, they might not have lost the civil war. One great success of the Communist Party was to win the support of the peasants; they formed the vast majority of members of the People's Liberation Army. The land reforms in Taiwan turned tenant farmers into owners of their own land and led to greater economic equality. The government paid as compensation to the landlords stocks in state-owned enterprises.

What saved the KMT was the Korean War and Mao's decision to send thousands of Chinese 'volunteers' to fight on the North Korean side — against the advice of Defense Minister Lin Biao. Lin argued the new state was too weak to take on one of the world's two superpowers. Suddenly, the United States changed its view of the value of Taiwan. The island became its 'battleship' in the western Pacific and part of a defensive ring from South Korea and Japan to the Philippines. It it is a strategic view Washington has retained until today. To support Taiwan, the US started a major program of economic aid. Between 1951 and 1965, it provided $1.5 billion aid, equivalent to Taiwan's budget deficit during that period. It was essential to enable a government burdened with a flood of people and a heavy defense budget to find its feet.

In 1953, the government announced its first four-year plan to develop industry and produce at home goods it was spending foreign exchange to import. It developed manufacture of textiles, foodstuffs, plywood and fertilizers. Like South Korea and Singapore, with low wages and efficient infrastructure, it attracted companies from Europe and North America to move production of labor-intensive goods. From the 1960s, the country began to export these goods to foreign markets. In 1965, it opened the Kaohsiung Export Processing Zone (EPZ), the first in Asia and the model of dozens of such zones in China and elsewhere. In the 1960s, Taiwan's economy changed from one reliant on agriculture to one based on industry and trade. Children of farmers moved to work in factories in Taipei, Kaohsiung and other cities. It became one of Asia's 'four little dragons', with South Korea, Hong Kong and Singapore.

Living standards rose dramatically. This was possible only because, under Mao, China was an economy closed to the West. It had limited foreign trade, most of it with other socialist countries. In the 1980s, Taiwan began to climb the technological ladder and move into electronics and computers. That is how it was when I arrived in 1981. An exporter of consumer goods to Japan, North America and Europe. Taiwan had started the process of upgrading itself. At home, its colleges and universities trained people in the new scientific and engineering skills. Abroad, it aggressively recruited Taiwan graduates of foreign universities, especially in the United States, to return and work in the new hi-tech companies.

After I moved to Taiwan, one thing that struck me was the absence of China. There were no goods or people from the Mainland, and residents of Taiwan were not allowed to go there. When we read the newspapers, there were stories about Tokyo and Toronto, Paris and Philadelphia but almost none about our giant neighbor and the world's most populous country only one hundred sixty kilometers across the Strait. From working at the United Daily News, I knew the stories we read about China were carefully selected and edited—only bad news, about floods, fires, accidents, corruption and internal Communist Party power struggles. When I chatted with Taiwan friends, I found they knew as little about China as I did.

In 1980, I had the opportunity to make a tourist visit from Hong Kong to Beijing. I had introductions to two foreigners living there. One was a British lady working for a trading company. She lived in a room in the Beijing Hotel; it had no lock, 'because socialist China is safe and no lock is needed'. Her boyfriend was a Beijing resident who came to visit her there. While he was there, visits from the staff increased. They entered the room without knocking and asked, "Do you need more hot water in your thermos flask? Is the room warm enough? Shall I change the sheets?" They did not like a romance between a Chinese person and a foreigner and did their best to discourage it. One day she took me to a local restaurant, where we ate meat balls. About thirty diners, men and women indistinguishable with short hair and blue cotton-padded jackets, had, I think, never seen Big-Noses. They crowded round the table and stared at us eating; they were not hostile, only curious. Not speaking Chinese then, I did not know what to say. Fortunately, my friend spoke it well and exchanged pleasantries with them. The other foreigner was Fox Butterfield, the first reporter of The New York Times to work in China since 1949. In 1982, he published *China: Alive in the Bitter Sea*, the first book written by the first foreign reporter to have lived there after the revolution. We sat in the cavernous restaurant of the Beijing Hotel; we were the only customers. We were greatly outnumbered by the staff, who kept coming and going to see what we were up to. A complete ignoramus, I was enthralled by Butterfield's description of this closed country. By comparison, living in Taiwan was so 'normal.' You could spend as much time as you wanted with Taiwan people; if you wanted, you could live with a local family. Such a trip as I had made to Beijing was impossible for a Taiwan person. His government would not permit him or her to go, nor would the Mainland give him entry.

Finally, in 1987, the Iron Curtain began to lift after thirty-eight years. In one of several major decisions in the last year of his life, President Chiang Ching-kuo announced in October that Taiwan people could go to the Mainland for family reunions. In Chapter Four, we described the reaction of some of the earliest who made the journey. Soon a trickle became a flood. In the nearly forty years since, the economies of Taiwan and China have become inextricably linked. Today China is the biggest export market for Taiwan goods and services and the largest overseas destination for Taiwan investors. For four decades, the boy and the girl never exchanged a word. Now they are entangled in a messy and complex marriage; divorce would be hard, if not impossible.

This transformation happened because Deng Xiaoping reversed the policies of Mao Zedong. In the early 1980s, China created four Special Economic Zones, modeled in part on the Kaohsiung EPZ, with privileged terms for outside companies. First to come were investors from Hong Kong; during the Maoist period, they had kept open lines of communication, mainly with Mainland entities in Hong Kong; they felt comfortable enough to invest there. They were followed by companies from Japan, South Korea and Taiwan. The Taiwan government said that, between 1991 and the end of 2021, it approved 44,823 projects of investment in China worth $198.28 billion. The real figure was probably higher. Fearful of restrictions by the Chinese or their own government, Taiwan firms set up subsidiaries in the Caymans, the British Virgin Islands or Singapore and made investments through these subsidiaries. The early investors from Taiwan made textiles, foodstuffs and low-technology products; these were low-risk, with limited value of intellectual property that could be copied or stolen. Many prospered from the low land and labor costs, encouraging others to come.

In 1994, I went to Tianjin to see one of the most successful of these early entrants—Kang Shi Fu (Master Kung), a maker of instant noodles. He had opened a factory there in 1992; by 1994, it sold 200 million packets across China. The Taiwan factory managers explained it was an ideal arrangement. Most of the workers were not from Tianjin but from outside the city; they lived in onsite dormitories built by Kang Shi Fu. "Their reason for working here is to earn money," one manager said. "Their families and social life are elsewhere. So they are willing to do overtime whenever we ask, including weekends." Wages were a fraction of those in the company's plants in Taiwan. As Chinese, the company's chefs understood well the tastes of Mainland consumers.

The manager explained their remarkable arrival in China. "After the crackdown in June 1989, flights leaving Beijing were full and those arriving were empty. That was the moment our founders (four brothers from southwest Taiwan) decided to come. They saw the opportunity. They were given a red-carpet welcome." The company hit the jackpot. It has since then become one of the biggest producers of instant noodles in China. In 2012, the overall market hit a record 44 billion packets—an astonishing 34 for each Chinese. Several factors explain Kang Shi Fu's success. One was first-mover advantage: creating tastes that suited Mainland palates: aggressive advertising and promotion, including collector's cards of heroes from the *Water Margin* inside the packets. The firm also benefited from change in lifestyles in the Mainland, as everyone became 'busy'. Instead of having a meal at home, the office canteen or a restaurant, people needed to eat on the move—in a car, a bus, a train or on a park bench as they headed back to the office. You can eat a plastic bowl of noodles anywhere. The success of Kang Shi Fu encouraged other

Taiwan firms to invest in the Mainland, including those with high levels of technology. Some exported the entire output of their Mainland plants, others sold part or all of it in the Chinese market.

Taiwan people had advantages over other investors. One was that they spoke Mandarin—most Hong Kong, Macau and Overseas Chinese businessmen could speak it also, but not with the same fluency. At meetings with the local mayor and Communist Party chief, they could pick up every nuance and meaning, even if not stated. Another was that they had grown up in a one-party Chinese state. "The Chinese communists and the Kuomintang are children of the same father, the Soviet Communist Party," one Taiwan investor told me. "While the KMT has greatly evolved now, the two parties have similarities." So they were often better equipped than Western or Japanese competitors to understand how the system worked and obtain the desired land, loan or approval.

But this closeness was also a weakness. The Chinese official felt closer to them and could demand a gift or favor for which he would not ask a German or a Japanese. Their greatest weakness is that they are not 'foreigners'; they have no protection from an embassy or consulate. Beijing considers them 'Taiwan compatriots'. In a dispute over land, money or personnel, to whom could they turn for help? In light of this, many Taiwan companies chose to invest close to their own compatriots. Two of the biggest clusters were in Kunshan, Jiangsu Province and Dongguan in Guangdong Province. Beijing even approved schools following the Taiwan curriculum in the two cities for children of Taiwan investors; this meant they could continue to live with their parents and not have to return to Taiwan to pursue their studies. These two cities were known as Little Taipeis. Let us hear the experience of Henry Chen, whom we met in Chapter Two. He worked in the mainland from 1990 to 2005, purchasing garments from factories there and selling them overseas. "Foreign buyers of Chinese garments used Taiwanese like me to purchase for them. My only financial investment was in an office in Xujiawei in Shanghai, which I later sold to another Taiwan businessman. He paid me in Taiwan dollars. I never did any financial transactions in the mainland, only in Taiwan. It was very troublesome to manage the production in mainland factories and ensure the right quality. I hired local people to supervise production. Staying in China was a mixed experience. Hotels in the big cities were fine. Once I was in a small town in Anhui Province, the hotel was terrible—with large rats racing each other across the floor and a broken sofa that stank. Those outside China could not imagine such conditions. He turned down all the ladies offered by his clients.

"As an unmarried businessman from Taiwan, I was a big catch, so I was very careful. I did not drink and everyone made fun of me. To avoid attracting attention, I never told people I was from Taiwan. I said I was from Fujian." The accent of Fujian people is close to that of Taiwanese.

The most extraordinary Taiwan investor in China is Hon Hai Technology Group (Foxconn). Founded in 1974, it has become the largest electronics manufacturer in the world, with revenue in 2022 of a record NT$6.627 trillion and net profit of NT$141.5 billion. It has manufacturing plants and R&D centers in more than seven countries around the world; it owns over 54,000 patents, according to the company website. In 2021, it ranked twenty-second on the Fortune Global 500 rankings. It makes electronic products for major American, Canadian, Chinese, Japanese and Finnish companies, including the Blackberry, iPad, iPhone, Kindle and Nintendo.

As its most important manufacturing center, China has been key to its success. Foxconn has a dozen plants in nine cities. In 1988, it opened its first factory there, in the Longhua District of Shenzhen. When I went to have a look, I realized that it was a city more than a factory. Covering three square kilometers, the site included fifteen plants, worker dormitories, swimming pools, a fire brigade, a hospital, bank, restaurants and shops. About a quarter of the workforce lived in the dormitories. At the time of my visit, there were more than 200,000 people working there. Another 'city' is in Zhengzhou, capital of Henan Province, with more than 300,000 workers. It produces most of Apple's iPhones and is called iPhone City. By 2020, Foxconn in Zhengzhou had become China's largest exporter, accounting for 60 percent of the total trade volume of Henan, the country's third most populous province. These plants were the perfect 'marriage' of Taiwan technology, management and global market access with China's unlimited supply of cheap, diligent and skilled workers.

A story no less remarkable is that of Taiwan Semiconductor Manufacturing Company (TSMC), the world's most valuable semiconductor company and the largest independent dedicated semi-conductor foundry. Its revenue in 2022 was NT$2,264 billion, an increase of 42.6 percent over 2021.

Its founder was Morris Chang, a Chinese born in Ningbo, Zhejiang Province, in 1931. Educated in Hong Kong and Shanghai, he moved to the US in 1949. He studied at Harvard University and the Massachusetts Institute of Technology. He worked for twenty-five years at Texas Instruments, rising to group vice president for its worldwide semiconductors. While he was in the US, the Prime Minister of Taiwan invited him to come to the island to develop its semiconductor industry. In 1987, he set up TSMC in Hsinchu, with $220 million in capital, half from the government and half from outside investors, including

Philips Electronics of the Netherlands. Chang's business model was to manufacture chips designed by other companies. His early customers included telecomm pioneers Broadcom and Qualcomm, graphics powerhouses Nvidia and ATI and mobile device innovator Marvell. The credit for the great success of the company must go to Chang and his colleagues, dedicated and highly skilled, but also to the government. It identified this sector as one with great potential, suitable for the engineers and conditions of Taiwan, and head-hunted a person even though he had no family connection to the island. The initial government investment was critical. It also created the Science Park in Hsinchu to provide the optimal conditions for TSMC and similar companies. It has set up two other Science Parks, one in Taichung and one in Tainan.

The company's success and global market have made it expand production outside Taiwan, including the Mainland, the United States and Japan; it is considering a foundry in Europe, probably in Dresden, Germany. These foreign projects involve investments of billions of US dollars. Chang insists none of them can match the efficiency and productivity of TSMC's plants in Taiwan, because of its density of talent, work culture and network of suppliers.

On September 15, 2018, he received from President Tsai Ing-wen the Order of Propitious Clouds, First Class, the first person from the business sector to receive this prestigious award. The government has given it to civil servants, civilians and foreigners for outstanding contributions to the country. "In 1985, the government recruited you to run the Industrial Technology Research Institute, a decision that altered the course of science and technology in Taiwan forever," said President Tsai. "The medal is for your contribution to Taiwan's IC industry, as well as development of the local high-tech sector. I greatly respect you and consider you a good friend. I often ask you for advice on how to promote national policies and have learned a lot from you."

Chang replied TSMC was the world's largest contract chipmaker and a very successful company. "It still faces still competition from firms in several countries such as the US, China and Japan, which are motivated by rising nationalism. The local industry also faces a shortage of resources, including water, land, electricity and talent. The government should give the tech sector the support it needs to prosper."

Kao Wei-bang is a highly trained chemist with degrees from universities in Taiwan, the US and Canada. In 1974, he returned to Taiwan to become chairman of a company specializing in fiber-reinforced polymer (FRP). A shortage of labor in Taiwan forced him to set up a wholly owned factory in a development zone outside Beijing. In early 1998, it began manufacture of his specialty products; each month two to three containers left for the US. A year later, during Spring Festival, when his workers were absent on holiday, a rival company with strong official backing accused him of not paying its debts; it had no debts, said Kao. The rival raided the factory and took as much product as it could; what it could not take, it destroyed. Kao could not continue production and his customers deserted him. He sought redress through official channels, including agencies of the central government, but got nowhere.

Back in Taiwan, he and others with a similar experience set up in 2003 The Association of Taiwan Investors Who were Victims in China. He said China used threats of legal action and physical violence to infringe the legal rights of Taiwan investors, leaving them with no recourse. "In many cases, a joint venture partner steals your technology and leaves you with nothing." He cited official Chinese figures as saying that each year Beijing received an average of 2,800 complaints from Taiwan companies. Only a fraction were settled. The most dramatic example came on May 1, 2009, when a Taiwan investor named Shen Bo-sheng (沈柏勝) went to Tiananmen Square in central Beijing. In despair at receiving what he considered unfair compensation from the Tianjin government, he committed hara-kiri, by cutting his stomach open. Passersby were able to save him from death and take him to hospital. Stunned by this action on its doorstep, the Politburo ordered the Tianjin government to settle the case in two years. In May 2011, Shen finally received a financial settlement— but it was less than 10 percent of what he had demanded. Kao's advice to his government and companies: do not invest in China nor become dependent on it.

I asked Taiwan people how common was the experience of Kao and Shen in China. "There have been sad cases," said Mary Liu, a schoolteacher. "A small investor loses money in China, for whatever reason. He takes a local mistress; his wife and children abandon him, so he loses his assets here. He cannot return to Taiwan. Larger companies are better equipped and can establish good relations with the local government. They are better able to protect their intellectual property." The consensus was that the golden era for Taiwan firms lasted about twenty years from the early 1990s. At that time, Mainland firms had a low level of technology, capital and management and lacked the experience and knowledge of Taiwan companies in export markets. But, by the late 2010s, these comparative advantages were being lost. That left only Taiwan firms with a high level of technology and niche products as welcome. My friend Henry said he left the Mainland market in 2005. "Conditions became impossible and they imposed too many restrictions on us. Many Taiwan businesses have left the Mainland. They are no longer useful there."

At the peak, as many as two million Taiwan people were living in the Mainland, including families. That was nearly ten percent of the island's population. They included not only those who had set up their firms and worked in Taiwan firms but also many in multinational companies. These firms needed production and sales managers, accountants, lawyers and other specialists. With their language and cultural skills, Taiwan people were well suited for these jobs. Working in a foreign company, especially a large one, gives you a measure of protection in the event of a dispute.

I had the opportunity to meet some of these Taiwanese residents. Always friendly, they were less forthcoming than they would have been at home. When I asked what problems they faced in their work, they did not like to be too specific. "You need good guanxi (關系, relations) with local officials. We depend on them," one said. European, American and Japanese companies were more willing to criticize Chinese policies openly; public debate was part of their strategy. But Taiwan firms preferred, I think, to resolve matters in private.

From the large number in the Mainland in the 1990s and 2000s, I assumed a majority were making profits. They had larger apartments and more living space than at home; they had domestic servants. Family separation was an issue. Outside Kunshan and Dongguan, there were no schools for Taiwan children. American, European and Japanese parents had more education options for their children. As a result, many Taiwan wives and children lived at home. Some of the husbands took local mistresses; this led to many family tragedies. In Shanghai, I found Taiwan investors who had bought apartments and moved there; some had even sold their properties at home, giving them no return option. When there were elections in Taiwan, things became tenser. The residents said they would fly back and vote for the KMT, which offered better relations with Beijing than the DPP. What else could they say?

After six decades of prosperity, Taiwan's economy has become like those of Western Europe. Services account for about two thirds of GDP, industry about one third and agriculture less than two percent. There is a large middle class and Taiwan diaspora around the world that buys houses and apartments at home. The big cities are full of five-star hotels, niche restaurants, spacious bookshops and upmarket department stores full of imported goods. Travel agents offer tours by rail, bus, bicycle and hiking; you can visit tea gardens, hot spring resorts and nature parks and live in the comfortable homes of farmers. Since 1995, Taiwan has offered National Health Insurance, providing free or low-cost care. There is also a flourishing private health sector. Some people complain that, when they need operations, Taiwanese who live abroad fly in to have the procedure done free-of-charge and then fly back home. Living abroad, they do not contribute to the economy.

Tourism is a big industry. A record 11.8 million visited in 2019, the last year before Covid. The government aims for six million in 2023 and 10 million by 2025. They come from China, Japan, Hong Kong, South Korea, India, Southeast Asia, with a smaller number from Europe and North America.

The Asia financial crisis of 2007-08 severely cut the number of tourists to Taiwan. At that time, I was staying in a hotel in Kaohsiung and came down to the restaurant for breakfast. The only guests there were large tour groups from the Mainland. I asked the lady next to me if this was her first visit to Taiwan. "I am from Shanghai. I have visited every province of China and wanted to see this one. We are having a good time with the food and the sites. We will be reunified soon." I could see the young waiter behind her grimacing as he served coffee and croissants.

When the group had left and boarded the bus, I asked the waiter for his thoughts. "We have no tourists at the moment except for these Mainlanders," he said. "We are grateful for the business. But I find it hard to hear much of what they say. We want the people's money but not the people (我們歡迎人民幣，不歡迎人民)."

He expressed the view of many Taiwan people who found it hard to accept the uncouth language and manners of some Mainland visitors, usually in low-cost tour groups. "They talk loudly on their mobiles, some spit and leave their hotel rooms open as they walk from room to room," he said. "People in other countries have a similar bad impression of this kind of Mainlander. But it is worse here, because they treat this as their own country and are not as restrained as they would be in France or the United States. A friend was at the top of Alishan, one of the most popular spots for both Taiwan and foreign visitors. When a Mainlander spat, my friend criticized him, saying, "You can do that at home but not here. It is not acceptable." The man replied, 'After we take it back, it will be.' "

10

Dance, Sculpture & Film

It was February 2017 and we were sitting in a booth at the Taipei International Book Exhibition (TIBE). We had organized a news conference at 2:00 p.m. to promote the book on the two Palace Museums we described in Chapter Eight. Two o'clock passed and no one entered the booth. After ten minutes, a middle-aged man arrived and sat down.

"Welcome," I said. "Allow me to tell you about our new book."

"No, let me see your hand first," he said.

He got up and examined the palm of my right hand.

"Not good, not good. You need to change your diet. You must eat garlic four times a day and drink a lot of soyabean." He started to give detailed culinary advice; evidently, he had no interest in the book. We listened politely. After ten minutes, he left. No one else came. So ended my worst-ever book presentation. I had only myself to blame. Such events need careful preparation; you must work with the organizers and do advance publicity. In a rush, I had done neither. My wife's comment: "This was a lesson in Buddhism, to teach you how unimportant you are."

That was my low point of several years' attendance at the TIBE. There were two high points. One year I wanted to give a book in person to President Ma Ying-jeou who was coming to open the event. I asked a friend at the Ministry of Culture for advice. She showed the route the President would take through the site after his speech.

"Here is a space so narrow his bodyguards will have to walk behind him," she said. "You can give him the book there." We followed her advice and waited for him. As he came down the space, I stepped out, handed him the book and bowed. A seasoned politician, he accepted it, smiled and said, "Thank you." We took a photograph of this precious meeting with the President. An unscheduled meeting with the head of state would have been impossible, of course, in the PRC and, indeed, in most countries in the world. But we could do it in Taiwan.

The other high point was a presentation organized with the help of Joint Publishing (JP), my publisher, on the main floor of the giant hall where the TIBE is held. We had an audience of about forty people; they were lively, full of questions and bought many copies; one invited us out for dinner that evening. Such exchanges are a great pleasure of being an author. But, again, there was no time to feel self-important. After the presentation, I walked a short way and found another JP author from Hong Kong. A singing star, she had written a book about how her three children had gained admission into famous universities in the US. There was a long queue in front of the table where she was sitting; everyone wanted a signed copy — and even no need for a presentation. Fame on the stage and getting into Stanford University — what more does a reader want? I could hear the Buddha whispering in my ear: "you think you are somebody?"

The TIBE attracts about 600,000 visitors and is the biggest event of the year for Taiwan publishers; they prepare book presentations months in advance. In 2017, there were 621 exhibitors from fifty-nine countries. The country produces 40,000 titles a year, including about twenty-five percent translated from foreign languages, especially English and Japanese, as well as comics and cartoons.

Taiwan ranks second in the world, after the United Kingdom, in the number of books published per capita—forty thousand a year for a population of twenty-three million. Like civil society overall, publishing boomed after the end of martial law in July 1987. The number of titles increased from 4,600 in 1980 to 16,200 in 1990 and 34,600 in 2000 and now 40,000 a year. The number of publishers has increased to more than seven thousand, of whom seventy percent have a staff of ten or less. This diversity of small publishers and independent bookshops has brought great vitality. Taiwan publishers export mainly to the Mainland and Chinese-speaking countries and little to the West. The Mainland market is difficult for foreign publishers to penetrate because of censorship and changing regulations. But Taiwanese agents are nimble and understand the market; they have good relations with Chinese publishers. An international study in 2014 found average per capita spending on books in Taiwan was 39.75 euros, ranking 17th in the world.

After the end of martial law, Taiwan started to compete with Hong Kong as the most free and most open publishing market in the Chinese world. Hong Kong had the advantage of easy access to and good contacts with the Mainland. Its publishers produced books that could not be sold in the Mainland but were popular with Mainland visitors; this proved to be a lucrative market. But, with the passage of the National Security Law (NSL) in Hong Kong in June 2020, the situation has changed. In books on history, current affairs, social sciences and other liberal arts, its publishers became uncertain what they can and cannot produce.

Publishing is an important part of Taiwan's 'soft power'. With exclusion from the United Nations and other international organizations, Taiwan has been losing its 'official' presence around the world. Instead, it is using its soft power—books, music, dance, theater, art, design and films—to spread its word overseas. The large Buddhist groups we described in Chapter Five are part of this soft power: they have membership and projects around the world. The Christian communities of Taiwan belong to global churches who pray and care for them. Not in the United Nations or the World Health Organization, no, but Taiwan has a deep footprint in many countries. The dramatic growth of civil society began after the lifting of martial law. What impressed me most was that this growth has resulted from the hard work of dedicated and visionary individuals; the state has played only a secondary role. In the Chinese-speaking world, Taiwan is the most free and most open society.

No visit to Taiwan is complete without a visit to a branch of Eslite, its most successful bookstore; it has more than forty branches across the island. It was founded in 1989 by Robert Wu Ching-yu. His business philosophy was that books alone were not enough to attract people and keep them in the store. So his branches offer a wide range of goods in addition to books, as well as coffee shops and restaurants. They also arrange talks, book presentations and other cultural events. Its first store was in Dunhua South Road in Taipei; in 1999, it became Taiwan's first twenty-four-hour bookshop. It has also opened an art gallery and subsidiaries selling kitchenware, food, drinks, home appliances and other items. It transformed the experience of browsing and buying books. When I visit Taiwan, I always like to visit a branch of Eslite, enjoy the rich selection of books and chat to the staff and other customers.

As a student in Taipei, I went to what was then the center of book-selling—dozens of shops along Chongqing South Road, south of the city's railway station. Many titles, as if they were falling off the shelves, but few places to sit—better to buy what you wanted and go elsewhere. Eslite's concept is the reverse: come in and do not leave. The shops are spacious and well lit, with places to sit and have a coffee. On January 1, 2006, it opened a new flagship store, with 8,000 square meters of floor space, in the Xinyi district of Taipei; it was the largest bookshop in Taiwan. Since then, this flagship store has attracted more than 200 million customers and offered books and magazines from more than 4,500 publishers in Taiwan and abroad—including mine. Sitting there one day, I asked a young man if he came to Eslite often. "Oh yes, when I have no girlfriend, I come here. It attracts a nice kind of woman and has a relaxed environment; you can talk to them easily," he said. Now Eslite has more than forty branches in Taiwan, most of them in the cities. In 2012, it opened its first branch outside the island, in Hong Kong; now it has six there. In November 2015, it opened its first Mainland branch in Suzhou, Jiangsu Province, and, in 2022, its first in Southeast Asia, in Kuala Lumpur. The success of Eslite, the shift to online sales and the changing habits of young readers have caused the closure of many of those traditional bookshops on Chongqing South Road.

A talk at one of Eslite's large Taipei branches is a dream for any author—he is guaranteed good promotion and a big audience. I tried for one, but lacked the necessary fame and connections (關系, guanxi) with the company. But they graciously arranged one in their branch in Tainan. It was not in a dedicated room but in the main sales area. We had an audience of about twenty, all polite and interested; among them was a lady from the office of the Taiwan government in Hong Kong whom I knew. At home on holiday, she was kind enough to make the journey to attend.

In trying to understand the traumatic events of 1949, I found the best teacher to be *Great River, Great Sea* by Lung Ying-tai, one of Taiwan's most famous authors. This book consists of stories of families broken up by the civil war. Over more than ten years, she had four hundred days of interviews with survivors in Taiwan and the Mainland, including Changchun, Nanjing and Shenyang. Published in 2009, it sold 100,000 copies in Taiwan and 10,000 in Hong Kong in its first month after release; sadly, it is banned in the Mainland. Her own family, from Hunan Province in south China, was a victim of the war. Her father was a KMT military police officer, who fled with his family to Taiwan. Born in 1952 in Kaohsiung, she grew up in poverty. She said her family had "lost everything", most importantly its family and social networks. I found in the book accounts similar to those I had heard from Mainland friends—leaving their hometown suddenly without saying goodbye and never imagining they would never return.

Lung has had a remarkable career. She has written over thirty books and held two official posts—Director of the Cultural Affairs Bureau of Taipei from September 1999 to March 2003 and the country's first Minister of Culture from May 2012 to December 2014. Some of her books and articles have appeared in the Mainland. In July 2005, with other intellectuals and like-minded business leaders, she established the Lung Yingtai Cultural Foundation with the aim of developing the civil society of Taiwan. Once I attended a speech she made in Hong Kong; she was a star. We queued to enter an enormous hall with several hundred places; every seat was taken. When she spoke, you could hear a pin drop. This is what a public intellectual should be like in the Chinese world, I thought, heard and read in Taiwan, Hong Kong and the Mainland. Alas, such is the animosity now between Beijing and Taipei there is little space for such an intellectual. Today could newspapers in Beijing, Hong Kong and Taipei print a critical analysis by Lung on the same day? I doubt it.

I had the good fortune to meet Lung twice, once when she was lecturing at Hong Kong University and once in Taipei. In May 2012, she surprised her family and friends when she agreed to become Minister of Culture; being a bureaucrat is not the usual choice of a free-thinking intellectual. What persuaded her was a sense of mission—to increase the share of culture in Taiwan's GDP from 4.9 percent to six percent, the level in Britain, by 2017. "I want to bring Taiwan's culture and creativity into the international market," she said. She cited the success of "Franz Collection", a brand of Taiwan porcelain that has sold products, including home decorative items, vases, tableware and jewelry, to sixty-six countries. Founded in 2001, it is based and has its R&D center in Taipei and its manufacturing in the Mainland.

To promote such companies, the government has set up five large artistic zones, two in Taipei and one each in Hualien, Chiayi and Tainan. One of the two in Taipei is in the Sungshan District, on an eighteen-hectare site that used to be a tobacco factory. "If it were in Hong Kong, there is a 99.9 percent probability the site would be sold or demolished," Lung said. "We have preserved it and used it entirely for artistic purposes, including design, visual arts, literature and performances."

Located in urban areas, the zones attract a large number of visitors, local and foreign. This brings a big audience for the firms that produce their work there. Lung held the ministerial post only until December 2014—two years and seven months. In resigning, she said she wished to care for her aging mother. Other factors, I think, were the bitter partisanship of politics and media in Taiwan—defending your policy initiatives in front of hostile parliamentarians with no knowledge of the subjects you are talking about. The second time I met her in Taipei she had left the ministry; she seemed more comfortable, with the freedom to which she was accustomed. Taiwan, and the Chinese world as a whole, is the richer for her many books and commitment to public life.

The most famous example of Taiwan's soft power in the

world is Cloud Gate, a dance troupe founded in 1973 by Lin Hwai-min. It was the first professional modern dance company in the Chinese-speaking world. It has performed in North America, Europe, Russia, Southeast Asia and Mainland China and has a global reputation. Its nickname is the 'Name Card of Taiwan'. The most remarkable testament to its popularity came in the spring of 2008. On the morning of February 11 that year, in the middle of the Lunar New Year, a fire devastated its studio and warehouse complex on the northern outskirts of Taipei. It destroyed the props, costumes, scenery and office equipment. Lin's responded, "The fire was a test from God. He must think Cloud Gate is still very young at thirty-five and can tackle a new challenge. We are ready for it." By the end of 2014, more than 3,700 donors gave $21.6 million, enabling the troupe to lease the former Central Radio Station overlooking the Tamsui River in New Taipei City and build a dazzling new center, its home today. The donations came both from Taiwan and overseas.

Lin was born in February 1947 in southwest Taiwan into a highly educated family. His father had a law degree from Tokyo Imperial University and his mother had graduated from Tokyo Economics College. Lin was educated at a Catholic secondary school and National Chengchi University in Taiwan; then he studied journalism and writing at the University of Missouri and University of Iowa in the United States. He also enrolled in a summer course at the Martha Graham Center of Contemporary Dance in New York. He could have become a famous author and journalist — but he chose modern dance. His curriculum vitae is typical of the diverse identity of Taiwan people. "My story has all along been a mixture of Taiwanese-Chinese, Western and Japanese influences," he said.

I had the privilege to meet Lin in the spring of 2017 in Macao, where Cloud Gate was performing *Rice*, a work he had choreographed. All of us in the room with him were conscious of being in the presence of a rare talent, a pioneer who had created dance performances inspired by Taiwan history, life and culture. In the Chinese world, he was a first. In addition, he is openly gay—a rarity in Asia. He explained he was inspired to write *Rice* after a visit to Chihshang, in the East Rift Valley of Taiwan, in 2011. It is famous for the high quality of its rice. "The moment you step into the fields, you drop everything," he said. "It is healing. I thought, "Would it not be nice to have Chihshang as a setting for dance? It is truly spectacular."

The seventy-minute piece describes the life cycle of rice and the love and labor of those who grow it. The music includes Hakka folk songs, Japanese compositions, Italian arias and classical works by Richard Strauss and Camille Saint-Saens. It premiered in Taipei on November 23, 2013. Outside the theater, more than 10,000 people gathered in Liberty Plaza to watch a free broadcast; similar public viewings were available around the country. After the performance, Lin led the dancers outside to mingle with the audience. He wants to bring dance to as wide a range of viewers as possible. The troupe often performs in schools and public spaces to reach those who cannot come to a theater.

Later, I visited the Cloud Gate Theater that was built after the fire. It is a striking location. Overlooking the Tamsui River, it opened officially on April 24, 2015. What an impressive location—next to the Hobe Fort built in 1886 and Taiwan's first golf course that opened in 1919. It has four performing spaces—a four hundred-seat main theater, two studios and one thousand-person capacity outdoor space. The theater is green in colour, built with green steel and set amid green grass, to blend with its surroundings. The troupe planted an additional two hundred trees on the property. It has become a popular public space.

When the troupe is not performing, visitors attend tours and rehearsals, take classes and enjoy picnics with a view over the river. Cloud Gate rents out the space for performances and music exhibitions. Open to the public free of charge, the space also has an outdoor sculpture exhibition, exhibitions at its gallery, and a restaurant and a bookshop. Each year, thousands visit, from Taiwan and abroad. "We want to do something different, not just be a dance troupe," marketing director Liu Gia-ye of the Cloud Gate Foundation, told me. All this reflected Lin's desire to share his love of art with the public and not reserve it for a small elite. It is a powerful expression of Taiwan's soft power and the dynamism of its civil society.

On a large hillside north of Taipei is another remarkable example of art for the public. This is the Juming Museum on 110,000 square meters. It opened in 1999 and is the largest outdoor art museum in Taiwan. Sculptor Ju Ming bought the wasteland in 1987 and spent twelve years turning it into a sculpture park. He donated more than two thousand pieces of his own works and personal collection for the public to see and enjoy. Among the figures are many with Ju's distinctive style—heavy, black material—resembling people in all shapes and forms. He made pieces out of bronze, stainless steel, painted wood, foam rubber and cast bronze. One series he called 'Living World', depicting people in many walks of life. It was a novel experience for me to walk over this wide expanse of open space and be so close to these distinctive pieces, to touch and admire them. Ju had the same vision as Lin Hwai-min—to bring his work as close to ordinary people as possible, not hide it in a museum or theater. Ju is the most famous sculptor Taiwan has produced; his works have been displayed in galleries, museums, hotels and department stores around the world. "We want the Juming Museum to become a museum for everyone, not just Ju Ming's museum," curator Joy

Lai told me. "We keep creating different visiting experiences for visitors to keep coming back." These include night shows, taichi yoga and pet days.

Ju was born in January 1938 and trained as a woodcarver. He used his skills on bronze, Styrofoam, ceramics and stainless steel and developed a successful crafts business. In 1968, he persuaded Yang Ying-feng, a master sculptor in Taipei, to accept him as an apprentice. In the 1970s, he sculpted water buffaloes, then widely employed on Taiwan's farms. Then he did a Tai Chi Series — outdoor statues of people practicing the art. In the 1980s, he began the Living World Series. "I belong to human society and know humans better than anything else," he said. "This subject allowed me more creative freedom, and it gave me an opportunity to look more deeply into the problems of life. I was hoping that I might be able to discover some truth during the process of creating sculptural works." He took his own life at home on April 22, 2023, at the age of eighty-five. According to the Taiwan media, he left only a simple note "我上樓了" ("I have gone upstairs."), with no explanation. The media said his body had been greatly weakened by a chronic illness, which he found very hard to bear.

Cinema is another art in which Taiwan has made its mark. The first time I noticed was when I saw Hong Kong film star Tony Leung playing a deaf-mute, one of four brothers in a Taiwan family just after World War I. He communicated with others, including his wife, mainly by writing. It was his familiar face that struck me first in a Taiwan film called *A City of Sadness* (悲情城市), made in 1989. Another thing I remember was the variety of languages used, including Taiwanese, Shanghainese and Cantonese, as well as Mandarin and Japanese; it was hard for a Big-Nose to follow. But I did recognize the setting — a town called Jiu Fen in northeast Taiwan. I had been there — a gold mining town but the gold had run out. I remember a small, old town clinging to the side of a mountain. It was not modern, which made it an excellent location for a film set in the late 1940s. The film was about the events of 1947, still largely a taboo subject in the 1980s. The director, Hou Hsiao-hsien, was smart. Martial law had ended only two years before; people were feeling their way in what could be expressed. The images in film stuck to the town and the family; they were greatly affected by the dramatic events going on outside, but we did not see the events in the film. I found it dramatic and realistic. It captured well the setting and complexity of that period. It was the first Taiwan film to deal with the events of 1947. I was not the only one to be impressed. In 1989, it became the first—of three—Taiwan films to win the Golden Lion award at the Venice Film Festival. Hou said of the film, "Everybody knew about the 2-28 Incident. Nobody would say anything, at least in public, but behind closed doors everyone was talking about it. The Incident was already known, so I was more interested in filming a time of transition and the change in a family during a change in regime. This was the main thing I wanted to capture." Hou went on to become one of the most successful Taiwan directors.

Cinema has been an important part of Taiwan's soft power. The government has recognized this by providing funds for the local film industry, to help it compete with films made by Hollywood, Hong Kong and other rivals and market its products in foreign markets. The industry produces about six hundred films a year and exports them to the Mainland and Asian and Western markets.

On the last Saturday in October 2019, more than 200,000 people marched through the center of Taipei in Taiwan Pride, the largest gay pride event in Asia. It had more people that Tel Aviv Pride in Israel, the biggest such event in the Middle East.

It attracted participants from all over Asia, most of them from countries where such a parade was not permitted. As I watched the event, I thought back to my years as a student in Taipei; such a parade was unimaginable. Martial-law Taiwan was a strict and conservative place. Most men had the short hair they had worn during their military service. In March 2023, a taxi driver told me that, during his service in the early 1980s, he was in a unit that scoured the streets for men with long hair. "When we found them, we took them to the police station for a haircut," he said. I do not recall seeing this—but it was in keeping with the time. When I lived there, I saw nobody, male or female, who looked gay, nor met anyone who said they were. It was like the societies of Europe in the 1950s and 1960s. Homosexuality was very well concealed; it was not accepted socially and had to be hidden from parents and family members.

So how did this transformation come about? Friends explained that after the end of martial law, Taiwan people could travel more easily to work, study and settle in foreign countries. There they encountered societies more tolerant of homosexuality. This encouraged gay people who had hidden their sexuality to come out. Public opinion at home remained conservative and hostile. In October 2003, the Executive Yuan (the Cabinet) proposed laws to allow same-sex couples to marry and adopt children, but they were opposed both by members of the cabinet from the DPP and lawmakers of the opposition KMT. So Parliament did not pass the laws. On November 1, 2003, the first Taiwan Pride parade was held; more than 20,000 people took part, from dozens of different groups. At the end of the parade, Ma Ying-jeou, then Mayor of Taipei and President from 2008 to 2016, gave a speech saying that, as an international city, Taipei should respect individuals of different groups and cultures. "Major cities in the world all have large gay communities," he said.

In 2011, eighty lesbians held a mass wedding; these marriages were not legally recognized. The breakthrough came in May 2017, when the Constitutional Court ruled the existing law was unconstitutional and same-sex couples should gain the right to marry. In a referendum the next year, Taiwan people voted 68 percent to 31 percent against marital rights for same-sex couples. But the government was bound to follow the court ruling. On May 22, 2019, President Tsai Ing-wen signed into law the right to same-sex marriage. Taiwan was the first country in Asia to recognize it. So we have come to where we are today.

Public opinion remains divided. In March 2023, David Chou, a manager in a kitchenware company said, "A majority of the public do not support gay marriage or the gay parade. Is Taiwan a democracy? I wonder if the government supports the gay parade as a way to attract thousands of people to come here. We are excluded from many global bodies, so the government is looking for international events to host here. Is Taiwan Pride one of them?"

Epilogue

This book describes my more than forty-year friendship with Taiwan. It is largely a happy story, of how a land has transformed itself from a single-party system under martial law into a diverse and pluralistic society that is one of the most open in Asia. It had made this transition without a coup d'état, military takeover, bloodshed or major social confrontations. Yes, at times there were fistfights in the legislature and political protests that drew tens of thousands of people into the streets. But, for the most part, these conflicts remained within the confines of the law. What is more, during these four decades, the economy continued to grow and develop, providing jobs and higher living standards for the island's people. Taiwan is by some standards the world's 20th largest economy and has routinely earned high marks in terms of economic freedom. Over the years, Taiwan's companies have invested billions of dollars at home and abroad — on the Mainland, in South and Southeast Asia and in Europe and the Americas. They have remained competitive against strong rivals in China, Japan, and South Korea and in the West. Taiwan citizens are blessed with other freedoms that make them the envy of many of their neighbors. As of January 2023, their passport entitled them to visa-free or visa-on-arrival access to one hundred forty-six countries and territories. This ranks the passport 32nd in terms of travel freedom, according to the Henley Passport Index. They can travel, work and study all over the world.

But, for all this progress, one issue, one existential issue, remains, the same as it was on that spring morning in 1981, my first day in Taiwan, when I watched young conscripts sing patriotic songs as they drilled on a military parade ground. That unresolved issue: what is the future of Taiwan? A province of China, an independent state or something between the two — the status it has enjoyed since 1949?

During the forty-two years since my first visit, there has been remarkable progress between the two sides — in trade, investment, and large-scale exchanges of people. Up to two million Taiwan people work and live in China and thousands of Mainland wives have moved to the island with their Taiwan husbands. In November 2015 in Singapore, the two presidents met for the first time. During Taiwan's martial law period, such a breakthrough was unimaginable. Putting emotion before analysis, I have long hoped the problem would solve itself, that the two sides would become so intertwined and their links so mutually beneficial that there would be no need to change anything. Both sides could live in peace. There were reasons for my optimism, particularly after comparing the situation to the division of Korea, another tragic legacy of the political settlements following World War II. Unity is out of the question; the people of North and South Korea live in different universes, mutually incomprehensible. When North Koreans escape and settle in the South, they find the greatest difficulty in adjusting to the 'promised land'; the southerners look down on them as poorly educated, backward and pre-modern, unable to use the internet or an ATM machine or read the Roman alphabet. By contrast, Taiwan and Chinese people adapt easily to life on the other side.

Hopes for a peaceful resolution were highest during the eight-year presidency of Ma Ying-jeou from 2008 to 2016; it was he who met President Xi Jinping in Singapore in that groundbreaking 2015 encounter. But even during that era, the two sides could not find a solution that both could accept. In 2016, the Democratic Progressive Party returned to power, and Beijing showed no interest in maintaining a dialogue.

Since 2016, political relations with the Mainland have deteriorated almost to the level seen in my early years in Taipei: no official relations between the two sides, plus a level of military brinksmanship not seen before. It is tragic indeed that the remarkable economic success of the two economies since 1980 has not created conditions that allowed a resolution. Since 2022, discussion of an attack on Taiwan or a blockade of the island, with possible military involvement by the United States, Japan, South Korea and other countries, has become an everyday subject for the media, think tanks and governments. Such discussions became more intense after Russia's invasion of Ukraine in February 2022.

During a visit to Taipei in March 2023, we found we could ask anyone about life under the threat of invasion. The question was as normal as asking about plans for lunch or the next vacation.

Answers were diverse: "it will never happen," "the time is not ripe now but perhaps later," and "we have nowhere to hide." I looked out of our hotel window and saw the streets bustling with life, well-dressed people hurrying to their offices, shops or factories. People enjoying one of the highest standards of living in Asia. Then I saw in my mind images of war. Such an eventuality would be tragic for the Mainland and Taiwan, as it has been for Ukraine and Russia. It would wipe out the progress I had seen over forty years.

I am encouraged by the hard work and optimism of the Taiwan people. Despite this existential risk, they continue their lives with the same energy and purpose as before. They go to the school, the office and the factory. On the weekends, they walk over the mountains and beaches and collect the plastic bottles, chip packets and cardboard boxes. They carry out charity missions to countries hit by earthquakes, floods and wars. Their semi-conductors power iPhones, computers, automobiles and passenger jets all over the world; without them, the global economy would seize up. They make me believe in hope and progress, that the two sides can find a way to live peacefully together. I look forward to more visits and to sharing in this progress, so that Taiwan can continue its remarkable contribution to the world. It will change others as it has changed me.

I dedicate this book to the people of Taiwan. It is they who made it possible. Since my first visit in 1981, they have treated me with warmth, friendship and humor. Some, of course, detested foreigners and said so in no uncertain terms. Others scolded me for mistakes of word usage and pronunciation and told me to study more before I opened my mouth again. In the martial-law period, a few said that I was a spy — but to qualify for such a role, you need connections, training and special knowledge, which I did not possess. I put it down to the atmosphere of the time; the government told its citizens to be on guard against people from outside and to suspect their intentions. Apart from the stabbing (Chapter One), I have always felt safe in Taiwan.

After the end of martial law, civil society developed rapidly and people became more relaxed. As civil liberties increased, people felt able to express themselves more freely. New newspapers and media opened, carrying different opinions. I found views becoming more and more diverse. Everywhere I met good manners and civil behavior. This reached an apex from 2006 to 2007, when I was commissioned to write the book on the Buddhist Tzu Chi Foundation; I spent most of my time with its members and volunteers. They were extremely well mannered and, in line with the instructions of Master Cheng Yen, reluctant to criticize others — even when it was merited. This was a remarkable universe.

In Taiwan, we met Hong Kong and Mainland people who

had moved and settled there. "You idealize Taiwan people too much," one Hong Kong migrant said. "That is in part because you are white. Best is to be American. Visiting and studying here is fine. But you are not competing with them for jobs, housing and opportunities, as we are. Then you see a different face, more inward-looking and protective of their own interests. Do not get carried away."

He and his wife had given up good jobs in Hong Kong to move to Taipei and open a boutique coffee shop near National Taiwan University. They served excellent food and coffee, but found it hard to make a living against the intense competition of other eateries and a landlord who was not so cooperative. To each person, his own experience and response.

Taiwan is a complex society, with many different opinions, especially about history. I ask readers to forgive me for not reflecting all this diversity and complexity. This is a book that describes my personal experience, the people I met and what I saw. It is not a complete history of Taiwan since 1981 — that would be a greater and more difficult project I leave to those wiser and more qualified than I.

The main sources for this book were the letters I wrote from Taipei between 1981 and 1983; articles I have written about Taiwan over these four decades; countless meetings with Taiwan people, in formal interviews and in social contacts in homes, coffee shops, bars, restaurants, beaches and on the slopes of mountains.

We must especially thank Cindy Shyu: Erwin Shyu:, Bob Wang, Henry Chan, Ivan Hsu, Emily Chang, Master Cheng Yen and her disciples, especially Rey Her and Lai Rei-ling, Paul Chang; my former colleagues at China Economic News: Chou Kung-shin, former director of the National Palace Museum, and her colleagues Yvonne Liang, Bill and Audrey Kazer and

Christine Yuan Winter.

I also used material from the websites of government departments, companies, schools, universities and other institutions.

For Chapter Three on Taiwan and Japan, we used:

"李登輝訪日秘聞", 王輝生, *The Secret Visits of Lee Teng-hui to Japan* by Wang Hui-sheng, Vanguard Books, Taipei, second edition September 2020

Wealth Magazine, Taiwan 22/12/2022 (財訊雙周刊，臺灣) on 'Taiwan-Japan Forum' in December 2022

"快讀臺灣史" 李筱峰， 玉山社 2002 年 *Quick History of Taiwan* by Li Xiao-feng, published by Yushan Publishing Co of Taipei in 2002: we used material from this book in several chapters.

Ministry of Culture website on Yoichi Hatta: https://www.moc.gov.tw/en/information_130_75059.html

For Chapter Five on the Presbyterian Church of Taiwan and the Taiwanese language, we used:

Official history of the Presbyterian Church of Taiwan, published in February 2008 (認識臺灣基督教長老教會)

Public Statements of the General Assembly of the Presbyterian Church in Taiwan, first published in 1991 and fourth edition in 2002

Stories of Chinese Christianity — George Mackay

https://bdcconline.net/en/stories/george-leslie-mackay

For Chapter Six, we used:

Democracy's Dharma — Religious Renaissance and Political Development in Taiwan by Professor Richard Madsen, University of California Press, published 2007.

Tzu Chi — Serving with Compassion — by Mark O'Neill, John Wiley of Singapore, published 2010.

Websites of the four Buddhist institutions

Also, the 2-28 Memorial Museum, Taipei.

For Chapter Eight:
The Miraculous Story of China's Two Palace Museums published in
Chinese and English by Joint Publishing of Hong Kong, 2016.

ABOUT THE AUTHOR

Mark O'Neill was born in London to a Northern Irish father and an English mother. He was educated at Marlborough College and New College, Oxford and became a journalist, working in Washington DC, Manchester and Belfast, before moving to Hong Kong in 1978. He has lived in Asia ever since, working in Taiwan, India, China, Japan and Hong Kong. Since 2006, he has concentrated on writing books. In 2023, Earnshaw Books published "*Out of Ireland*". This book on Taiwan is his sixteenth.